THE EVOLUTION OF A COMMUNITY

Reports of
The Institute of Community Studies

THE EVOLUTION
OF A COMMUNITY

*A Study of Dagenham
after Forty Years*

★

Peter Willmott

LONDON
ROUTLEDGE & KEGAN PAUL

First published 1963
by Routledge & Kegan Paul Limited
Broadway House, 68–74 Carter Lane
London, E.C.4

Printed in Great Britain
by W. & J. Mackay & Co. Ltd., Chatham

People interviewed in this survey have been given
fictitious names and other details about them have
been changed in order to conceal their identities. The
names of roads have also been altered

S400/200/3/23/66

CONTENTS

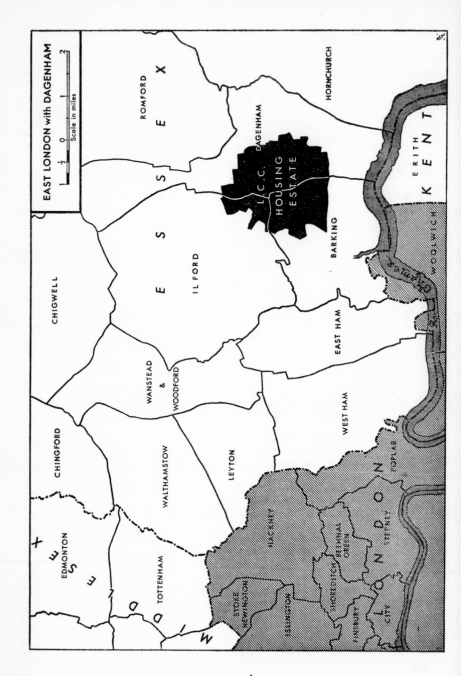

EAST LONDON with DAGENHAM

Scale in miles

vi

INTRODUCTION

In the past half-century many thousands of families have moved, under the benevolent guardianship of local councils, from grimy Victorian streets in the inner districts of Britain's towns and cities to new housing estates on the outskirts. They have found the new life there very different, as a series of sociological studies have amply demonstrated in recent years. The research carried out in old districts and new has been extraordinarily consistent in its findings. As a result, one can talk about life in the 'old working-class communities' or the 'new council estates', knowing that, despite variations, the descriptions probably hold, in essence at least, for similar types of area all over the country.

The older districts studied include Barton Hill in Bristol, St. Ebbe's in Oxford, Crown Street and 'Ship Street' in Liverpool, Govan in Glasgow, Bethnal Green in London.[1] All these have three characteristics in common—they are largely one-class, they are near to the city centre, and many of their houses are, or were, 'slums'. Increasingly, the old homes in such districts are being replaced by new blocks of council flats, but the rest of the housing is nineteenth century—usually a maze of terraced streets of two- or three-storey houses, often overshadowed by the giant tenement blocks which were a product of late Victorian philanthropy. Industry is either in the thick of the district—breweries,

---

[1] See Jennings, H., *Societies in the Making*; Mogey, J. M., *Family and Neighbourhood*; Brennan, T., *Reshaping a City,* and *Family and Kinship in East London,* by Michael Young and myself; all these compare central districts with suburban estates. For studies of central areas alone, see Vereker, C., Mays, J. B., *et al., Urban Redevelopment and Social Change*; and Kerr, M., *The People of Ship Street.* Full references to all books and articles cited are given in Appendix 4.

small workshops, warehouses, and smoking factories ming-
ling with homes—or is close by. As well as the main shopping streets or markets that serve the area, it has a host of
small corner-shops and public houses.

Although in these neighbourhoods there are some new-
comers, the majority of residents have lived there for all or
much of their lives.[1] As a consequence of this stability,
most people have relatives close at hand. They also see them
frequently, mothers and their married daughters, in particular, often maintaining daily contact. Kinship, in other words,
plays a central part in people's lives; and it provides 'the
first line of defence in sickness, emergency and old age'.[2]
Apart from relatives, many of the other local residents are
acquaintances or friends of long standing; the community
is described as extremely 'friendly' or 'neighbourly'. There
is a good deal of mutual help and a general air of easy-going,
informal sociability, reinforced by the frequent casual meetings, in local shops, pubs and markets, and in the streets
themselves.

On the new estates, by contrast, the 'immediate family'
of parents and their young children is more isolated. The
housing is more spread out, and there are fewer, if any,
local shops or pubs. In the main, the relatives have been left
behind in the old districts, and so are naturally seen much
less often. Not only do people fail to make up for this by
seeing more of non-relatives; they are inclined to be sus-
picious of their fellow residents, sometimes describing them
as 'unfriendly' or 'standoffish'. A study of a London
County Council estate in Hertfordshire found noticeably
more mental illness amongst its residents than among people
in the country as a whole.[3] In sum, life is more strained, more

---

[1] In certain other kinds of inner district—examples are those near the London
main-line railway termini—the population is, of course, much more transient,
just as one section of the Crown Street district, studied in Liverpool, proved to
have a much more mobile population than the rest. Vereker, C., Mays, J. B.,
et al., op. cit., pp. 81–87.

[2] Jennings, H., op. cit., p. 108.

[3] Martin, F. M., Brotherston, J. H. F., and Chave, S. P. W., 'Incidence of Neurosis
on a New Housing Estate'.

Introduction

'reserved', more lonely than in the older districts—this is the impression one draws from these various inquiries.[1]

The influence of time

But these surveys all suffer from limitations, and one, above all, is crucial: time is left out. Most of the estates were new when they were studied, so that some important questions have remained unanswered. Are the isolation from kin and the aloofness from neighbours part of a new way of life altogether, or are they merely transitional? What social patterns evolve on housing estates when place and people have had time to settle down; how do they then compare with the 'traditional' communities? This book sets out to answer such questions for one estate—the London County Council's vast settlement in Dagenham, Essex, which was built between 30 and 40 years ago.

A generation has now grown up at Dagenham. The tenants who went in the 1920s and 1930s are grandparents, even great-grandparents, their children old enough to have themselves pushed prams along the same roads. The estate had been studied before, so that some comparative information was available. A survey by Terence Young, published in 1934, chronicled the estate's early growth,[2] and it had also been included, under the pseudonym of 'Oak Estate', in a survey of housing carried out by Mass-Observation in 1941–2.[3]

Another motive for choosing this particular estate was that, like Bethnal Green, the post-1945 estate of 'Greenleigh' and the middle-class suburb of Woodford—three places we had previously studied—it is part of East London.[4] This was an obvious advantage; Terence Young's earlier survey had shown that many of Dagenham's population were

---

[1] Apart from the housing-estate studies already referred to, see Kuper, L., 'Blueprint for Living Together'; Mitchell, G. D., et al., Neighbourhood and Community; Hole, V., 'Social Effects of Planned Rehousing'.
[2] Young, T., Becontree and Dagenham.
[3] Mass-Observation, People's Homes.
[4] See diagram on p. vi. The study of Woodford was reported in Family and Class in a London Suburb, by Michael Young and myself.

East Enders in origin, and if this turned out to be still true—as it did—then it would mean that many of Dagenham's residents, like those of Greenleigh, had originated in places like Bethnal Green itself. This made comparison much easier.

A third reason for the choice of Dagenham was that it is, in terms of town planning, such a monstrosity. Its design and layout offend most of the canons of urban planning, and it is commonly held up, among planners and architects, as a dreadful warning—a supreme illustration of how not to build a new community. Here, if anywhere, one might see how planning mistakes had warped the social life of a community.

The survey

The study that follows was not of the borough of Dagenham, but of the London County Council's estate there. Since there is some confusion, even among local people, about how to refer to the estate, it is probably as well to clear this up right away. The housing estate of 27,000 houses is owned and administered by the L.C.C., and the L.C.C. calls it 'Becontree'. The biggest part of the estate—over half of it—is in the borough of Dagenham; and over half the houses in that borough are on the estate. The remainder of the estate is in the boroughs of Barking and Ilford, so that tenants may live in any one of these three local authority areas. A few of those whose homes are in the last two boroughs assert that they live in 'Ilford' or 'Barking', but most say, with their neighbours in the borough of Dagenham, that they live at 'Dagenham'; this is, in fact, the official postal address of the entire estate. It is also the name by which it is generally known to other people. To most people, on or off the estate, 'Becontree' is the name only of a relatively small district around the station which bears this name. I shall call the estate 'Dagenham' or 'the Dagenham estate' throughout this book.

In the course of the research I talked to councillors and

officials of both the L.C.C. and the local councils to get their views; and wherever we went my colleagues and I observed, as carefully as we could, in shops, in parks, in streets, in pubs and cafés, the public lives of Dagenham residents. But most of the information for this survey comes from interviews with people in their homes. There were three main sets of these, which I refer to briefly here, a fuller discussion of the methods of the inquiry being set out in Appendix 1.

1. *The general sample.* This was a random sample of men and women living on the estate, drawn from the electoral registers. Out of 993 people called on by our team of interviewers, 116 refused to be interviewed, leaving 877 about whom information was secured. The big majority of those interviewed were married—78%. Another 9% were widowed (widows outnumbering widowers by six to one) and less than 1% divorced; 13% were single—mostly unmarried sons and daughters living with parents. The interviews were straightforward and relatively brief, providing some basic information about where relatives lived, how often they were seen and so on, and also something about work, neighbours, social class, and the like.

2. *The marriage sample.* A sample of 50 married couples with young children whom, with the help of Ralph Samuel, I re-interviewed at greater length. The couples were a subsample picked at random from the households in the general sample containing a married couple and two or more children under 15. The sample was chosen in this way so as to be comparable with similar groups—like them, mostly in their thirties—in Bethnal Green and Greenleigh.

3. *The tenants' sample.* This was a further group picked from the general sample for intensive interviews. Phyllis Willmott and I interviewed 20 people selected at random from the tenants (or wives of tenants) who moved to the estate with their children in 1930 or earlier. These were naturally older people, mostly in their fifties and sixties, who were asked about their earlier experiences of Dagenham and how it

had changed through the years. We also inquired about where their children were now living, how often they were seen and so on.

These three sets of interviews were carried out in 1958 and 1959. I returned to Dagenham at the end of 1961 to collect recordings for a B.B.C. broadcast about the estate, and interviewed once again some 30 families from the marriage and tenants' samples, together with a number of teachers, local government officials, councillors and so on. This visit, though brief, provided some further impressions to add to the material gathered earlier.

Information from these various sources is combined in the chapters that follow. My account is obviously a limited one. First, there are many aspects of life on the estate that are ignored. Most of the people in the general sample were husbands or wives, and the marriage sample, from whom so much of the detailed information comes, is entirely made up of married couples with young children. Other groups at Dagenham have been studied much less fully, or left out altogether—the life of adolescents, for instance, is not covered at all.

Secondly, Dagenham's patterns of life may not be the same as those of other new communities. It is obviously in some ways unique, and it would therefore be wrong to assume that the new settlements built since 1945 will duplicate its experience exactly. Two final caveats—the validity of this survey, like others, depends on the assumption that people's behaviour is as they report it; it may not be. And, in trying to interpret what is happening at Dagenham, I have in places gone beyond the statistical evidence. Although I have tried to guard against my own biases in doing so, the danger that they may have distorted the account is an obvious one.

*   *   *   *   *

This study was financed by a grant to the Institute of Community Studies from the Leverhulme Trust, and in the

Introduction

later stages by the Joseph Rowntree Memorial Trust, as part of its general support for the Institute's work.

Thanks are due to my colleagues at the Institute for their help and advice, in particular to my wife, Phyllis Willmott, who collaborated closely in the interviewing, analysis and final writing. The London County Council co-operated fully with the inquiry; I am grateful to its officers, and to those of the Essex County Council and the Dagenham Borough Council. Among the latter, special mention must be made of Dagenham's Chief Librarian, John O'Leary, and, among his staff, of Leslie Cannon, who helped in countless ways. I am indebted to the following people, who made useful suggestions on the book in draft: Sir Alexander Carr-Saunders, Euan Cooper-Willis, Oliver Cox, Professor D. V. Donnison, Herbert J. Gans, Geoffrey Gorer, Margot Jefferys, Robin Huws Jones, Ernest Lenderyou, Ann MacEwen, Professor Charles Madge, Geoffrey Nicholson, John H. Nicholson, Michael Richardson, W. G. Runciman, Richard Rose, Graeme Shankland, Richard Thomas, Lewis Waddilove and William Wallace. And to Stephen Schenk, who helped with the direction of the general survey at Dagenham, and from whose erudition I have freely borrowed in writing this book.

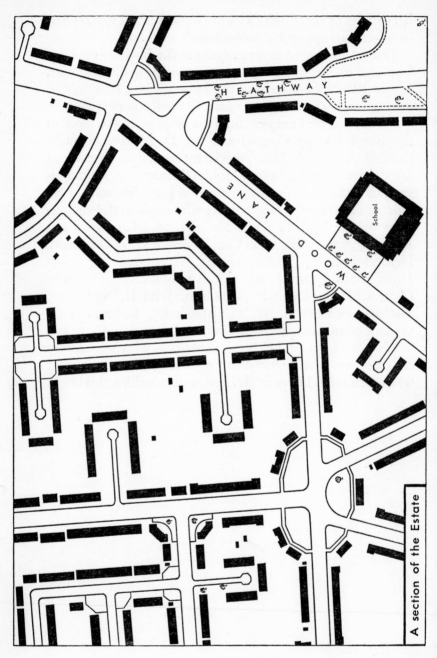

A section of the Estate

xiv

I

THE ESTATE AND ITS BEGINNINGS

THE visitor to Dagenham does not need to be told that he has come to a council housing estate. It has the stamp—the two-storey brick terraces, the geometric road patterns, the tame grass, the monotone air. The L.C.C. planners, it is true, have tried hard to avoid the characteristic uniformity, but with only limited success.

The first view is of endless thoroughfares lined with straight rows of little houses, though anyone who turns off the broad main roads will find some diversity in street layout. A number of roads have been deliberately curved, and as well as straight roads, short and long, wide and narrow, there are squares, crescents and 'circuses'. There are also many cul-de-sacs, known locally as 'banjos': the inhabitants thus taking an aerial picture of themselves—a 'banjo' is a short, narrow street which opens into a circle.[1] These attempts at variety are far from enough to remove the general effect of monotony: the same patterns of streets are reproduced again and again, and in the end it is the similarities that impress rather than the differences. In the words of one resident, 'You walk around the streets and it's more or less the same thing all the time'.

The sameness in the look of the houses themselves is partly to blame. Again the L.C.C. can point out proudly that there are as many as 91 different house-types on the estate, and if some of the minor differences are apparent

---

[1] Some of these street designs, including a number of 'banjos', can be seen from the diagram opposite.

only to the maintenance men, there is still some variety discernible to the casual observer. For one thing, there is the surprise of 200 'weather-board' houses, creosoted dark-brown in traditional Essex style. There are others in red brick, yellow brick, grey rough-cast, cement rendering—shortage of materials in the building boom of the 1920s helped to oust one kind of uniformity. There are low roofs with dormer windows and high ones without, slate roofs and tiled. There are arched, red-floored porches shared by adjoining houses, plain front doors opening on to white steps, ornamented neo-Georgian porticos. There are brightly coloured doors in contrasting reds and yellows and greens. Still, the boxes are very much alike in essentials—all two storeys high, with two or three bedrooms, sloping roofs, a small front and larger back garden. They were all built in the same era, to the same kind of budget, for the same basic purpose—and it shows. 'When you've seen one house on this estate,' one of the tenants said, 'you've seen the lot.'

Apart from these uniformities, Dagenham lacks visual contrasts because, like so many other estates, it is almost all houses. Not only are there few flats—they account for less than a tenth of all the dwellings—public buildings are also rare. There is not even a civic centre of any kind. A site was left by the L.C.C. for this purpose, in the hope that the estate would eventually become 'a township more or less complete in itself . . . within the jurisdiction of one single local authority'.[1] This did not happen, apparently because the Essex County Council and the boroughs in which the estate lay could not come to an agreement. The result was its continued partition—the estate is owned and managed by the L.C.C., and the local services provided by three borough councils—Dagenham, Barking, and Ilford. The civic centre of Dagenham Borough Council, which is re-

---

[1] The L.C.C.'s plan was for the site to house 'a shopping centre, markets, public buildings and so on'. *Report* by the Architect and the Director of Housing to the Housing (Building and Development) Sub-Committee, 25 February 1920.

sponsible for more than half of the estate area, is off the estate to the north-east. 'The "civic centre",' as one informant said, 'is near to a bus garage, but that's about all it is near.'

The estate has its schools, of course, squat and solid in pre-war council style, with outside lavatories, asphalt playgrounds and wire fencing. And the pubs: there are nine on the estate—long, low buildings, with huge echoing bars and lounges. Post offices are in obviously simulated Essex farmhouse style, with heavy oak doors. The shops are clustered in a dozen centres, each at a main road junction, surrounded by barricades of railings and wire-mesh; the safety-first posters on the wire seem as much as anything addressed (too late) to the planners whose plans helped to create the danger. As for the churches and church halls, they are red-brick spire-less blocks or grey asbestos huts.

These buildings have the unmistakable mark of their era on them—the estate has hardly any buildings older than 40 years or younger than 20. Apart from a handful of farmworkers' cottages which have survived, and stand out oddly amongst their neighbours, only two older houses remain. One, a farmhouse converted into the L.C.C. housing office, is hidden behind a tall wooden fence, a cluster of prefabricated huts, and the bric-à-brac of a maintenance depot. The other, an elegant manor house which serves as the local museum and central office for Dagenham Borough Council's libraries, stands tucked away behind a red-brick library and a rank of war-time air-raid shelters, now used as Council stores.

The net impression is of street after street of houses, mile upon mile of them. The estate seems unending; and it is, in fact, immense. Its 27,000 houses cover 2,700 acres—over four square miles. It is larger in area than many a London borough, more than three times the size of Bethnal Green, larger than Bermondsey or Poplar, Hampstead or St. Pancras. In population Dagenham is bigger than the postwar new towns. Crawley's planned population is 55,000,

Harlow's 80,000, Hemel Hempstead's 80,000 Cumbernauld's 50,000. Dagenham's population is over 90,000, larger than that of Lincoln or Bath, Doncaster or Burnley. It is the biggest housing estate in the world.

However much councils have been vandals themselves, they have not always been lucky with their sites; seldom can they have been faced with such a daunting topography as this. The terrain does not help in any way to offset the tedious architecture; indeed, the one vastly emphasizes the other. The two-storeyed rows march across the flat land, the uniform level of their roof-tops matching the evenness of the Essex countryside upon which Dagenham was built. Except for the Ford Motor Company's gas-holders, two shining columns that punctuate the horizon to the south, there is nothing in sight but the houses immediately at hand—no vistas, no perspectives, no slopes or distant hills.

The parks and open spaces are as flat as the rest of the estate. With houses showing them only their untidy backs, they have a bare, sad look about them. So, too, do the rectangular or triangular corner-sites with broken-down railings, the six-feet grass or gravel verges where yellow groundsel flourishes, the broad green stretches along the main roads. These blank ubiquitous patches help to give the estate a wasteland air.

It is not until one begins to look more closely at what people have done to the houses that the impression of sameness recedes a little. The place has 'weathered'; the tenants and time have between them taken off that raw look of new council housing. Most homes have privet hedges, now full and thick. The walls of many others have been softened by virginia creeper, jasmine or honeysuckle. There are trellis fences and thriving rose-bushes, rockeries and cherry-trees. Homes like these give the appearance of thousands of hands having smoothed over, and made more human, the original plans rolled out from County Hall. But the general atmosphere—of a vast flatness, openness and uniformity—is still overpowering.

How it began

At first sight, it looks as though Dagenham is entirely a creation of the twentieth century. But the area has a 'pre-history', which is explored and recorded with affection and scholarship at Valence House by Dagenham Council's Chief Librarian.[1] The story of the Benedictine Abbey at Barking, the flooding of the district in 1376, the rise and fall of the ancient manors of Valence and Parsloes—all these have been carefully chronicled. What is more, though few tenants can be aware of the fact, much of this past history is honoured in the names given by the L.C.C. to the estate's streets—in Parsloes Avenue and Fanshawe Crescent, for instance (after the family which owned Parsloes Manor for 300 years); in Bennett's Castle Lane (after the moated homestead occupied by Thomas Bennett in the seventeenth century); in Ford Road (named not after Henry but William, a local farmer who endowed an early nineteenth-century charity school).

The break came in 1919. Where the estate now stands was at that time quiet farmland, lying between the country village of Dagenham and the expanding outer-London suburb, as it then was, of Barking. This stretch of the Thames Estuary was treeless, with low, thin hedges and flat fields, mostly devoted to market gardening. Into this placid countryside, where smallholders grew their carrots and brussels sprouts for the London markets, came an unobtrusive representative of the London County Council, who, in Terence Young's words, was 'going about making discreet inquiries of the ownership of the fields, houses and other properties'.[2]

After the First World War, as in 1945, the L.C.C. had been faced with the urgent task of providing thousands of new houses, the bulk of them, if possible, outside the county, so as to reduce overcrowding and congestion inside.

[1] See, for instance, O'Leary, J. G., *The Book of Dagenham* and *Dagenham Place Names*.
[2] Young, T., op. cit., p. 34.

The biggest need was for new homes for people from the East End, since it contained, as the Council said, 'the most densely occupied and the most overcrowded areas, and generally the worst conditions in London'. 'The natural and necessary outlet', explained the L.C.C., 'was in an easterly direction from London, and the dense development in the intervening outer London districts made it necessary to go as far as Becontree to obtain an estate of a size sufficient for the requirements.'[1] The estate was intended to meet the bulk of London's urgent housing needs—the Council planned to build a total of 29,000 houses in its five-year programme after 1919, of which 24,000 were to be at Dagenham. This ambitious plan was held up, partly by economic setbacks, partly by reversals in Government policy, but building began in 1921 and went on, with ups and downs, into the 'thirties. To create from scratch what was virtually a large new town in just over a decade was an impressive achievement, in quantity comparing very favourably with the post-1945 new towns.

It was in the northern section that building started. By the end of the first year there were 465 houses, after the second 2,700, and after the third 3,296. In 1923 a second settlement was begun, in the south near the old village of Dagenham, and through the years the terraced houses stretched rapidly across the fields to meet each other and spread out to the furthermost edges of the site. By 1932 there were about 22,000 houses, and the completion of the estate was officially celebrated in 1935.

The first tenants

From what the older tenants told us, and from Terence Young's account, it seems as if people's experiences in the early years were much like those of migrants to the new crop of estates built since 1945. The new house, as always, had been the principal attraction to those who moved. 'The thing that pleased us most when we first moved here 30

[1] L.C.C. Minutes, *Housing Committee Report*, 22 June 1926.

years ago,' said Mrs. Powell,[1] 'was to have a house of our own, with electric light and a bathroom and a scullery with running water. We'd been in two rooms in Bethnal Green, with a tap and W.C. three flights down and shared with two other families. With all the cupboards and the stove and everything, I thought it was just like a palace.'

Then there was the garden. Mrs. Adams remembered the pleasure it gave her when her daughters were small: 'I had a little wooden table round by the side of the house. In the summer the girls had their friends in to play on the grass. They looked so sweet out there. I used to give them salad and something to drink. Sometimes when I look out of the window now I think of the little girls. Of course, it's all gone now—they've all grown up.'

The new-comers from London were also able to enjoy being 'in the country'. Their wistful recollections of this echoed those of other migrants to suburbs, both public and private, who so often find that when more and more people have made the same journey, the 'country' they valued so highly has vanished.

'It was different from what it is now. Really country, it was then. It was all market gardens; we used to get our vegetables straight from them. Wood Lane was just a winding narrow lane with cows.'

'We could walk for miles over the stiles to Rainham, over rhubarb and cabbage fields. Sometimes we went blackberrying, and we went across to the farm for our milk and eggs. It was all green fields then, really lovely, really country.'

The estate was, as people told us in familiar phrases, 'healthier', 'cleaner', 'more open', 'so much better for the children'. 'There was so much fresh air after all the smoke of London.'

The difficulties of the new-comers were familiar, too. People drew the contrast between their new life and the

[1] This, like the names given to other informants throughout the book, is fictitious; other details about people have also been changed in order to conceal their identities.

social atmosphere of the old district. 'It was a big wrench for me,' said one wife, 'because I'd always lived in the East End. It seemed as if we'd really come into the wilds.' And another said, 'It was terrible the first two years away from Mum. I longed to go back to Hoxton.'

Some of the early tenants also reported the same competitiveness between neighbours as has been observed in more recent studies. Mr. Gale said:

> 'When we first came down here people were making themselves out to be something they weren't. They tried to live up to the area. They'd mostly been living in just one or two rooms before then, and they thought they were it. They thought they'd show they were better than Mrs. Jones.'

'We came in 1925,' said Mrs. Hamilton. 'Everybody was trying to outshine their neighbours then. We'd all come from bad housing—two rooms and that sort of thing. When you saw your house you thought you were in a palace. You tended to show off a bit.'

The new estate was certainly a strange environment, especially while it was still being built. 'We were pioneers out here then,' said Mr. Ball; 'the place was like a wilderness. It was all muddy and empty. There were builders and trucks and railway lines and piles of bricks everywhere.' Mrs. Adams had an unpleasant experience. 'I went out for a walk and when I came back all the houses looked alike to me. I was in a terrible state—in tears. The workmen said, "What's the matter, ducks?" I said, "I can't find my house."'

> 'There wasn't a lamp-post in the street,' Mrs. Hamilton recalled. 'They were still building here when we came in and there were railway lines all up this street. There were no shops here then; you had to go over the level crossing and down to Church Elm Lane to get your shopping done. You went right up to your ankle in mud and slime in the winter. There were awful muddy holes in the road and the women used to pick up bricks from the building site as we went past and drop them in the holes in the road to give us stepping-stones for our feet on the way back.'

During the first decade residents also suffered in all sorts of ways from a lag between house-building and the provision of local amenities and local employment.[1] Terence Young pointed out that the L.C.C. '. . . had to see, of course, that gas, water, electricity and sewage disposal were adequate, but the onus of providing public and voluntary social services in the necessary amounts at the right time rested with other authorities. . . . Moreover, new industry did not move to the district in step with the increasing population, although industrial development was foreseen and planned. There was practically no increase until the Estate had been in existence for ten years.'[2]

One of the worst problems was education. The school-age population increased from 2,000 to 25,000 in a decade, and the schools could not keep pace. 'There were no schools when we came,' said Mrs. Kemp. 'My girl was six then, but as we came in August, she didn't start school until the following Easter. Alibon Road was full up and they hadn't built Hunter's Hall School till then.' This was by no means exceptional. Young gave some examples from different parts of the estate. 'School facilities were entirely lacking, at least within a reasonable distance from the new houses . . . in north Dagenham there were no schools close by. A number of the infants travelled the long distance to the Chadwell Heath Infants' School. . . . This soon became overcrowded. . . . The Dagenham village Infants' School during 1924–5 doubled its numbers and became full. Marsh Green School . . . added another 100 to its roll and had an excess of 60.'[3]

The second big difficulty was transport, all the more

---

[1] This has been frequently noted. White, for instance, in his study of housing estates, remarked on 'the defects of inter-war housing, with its shortsighted emphasis on mere housing and its lamentable failure to plan for social needs.' White, L. E., *Community or Chaos*, p. 21.

[2] Young, T., op. cit., p. 27.

[3] Young, T., op. cit., pp. 39–40 and pp. 58–59. Further education was also inadequate. Robson, W. A., reported in 1939, 'Evening institutes did not appear for some years, while those who want technical instruction must still travel some distance to the institutes of boroughs much nearer London or within the administrative county.' *The Government and Misgovernment of London*, p. 433.

important because there was so little local employment. The estate was poorly served by buses—there were at first no services linking the two areas in which building started—and until 1932, when the line was electrified and new stations provided, the trains to London, where most people still worked, were infrequent, slow, and even more overcrowded than they were later. Mr. Payne recalled what it was like.

'I had to get to work in Shoreditch at half past seven. It meant I had to get up at five and walk through the mud for 20 minutes to Dagenham Station. It was raw in the winter mornings, I can tell you. The trains were packed. Then it was a half-hour bus ride at the other end. If it hadn't been for the wife and the children, I don't think I'd have stuck it, to tell you the truth.'

Mr. Gale met the problem in another way.

'I was working in Poplar and if I'd been able to get a house there I'd have stayed. The trains were no good in those days and then there were the fares. I used to bike it every day. Hard work it was, especially in the cold and the rain.'

Most workers used public transport, inadequate and uncomfortable though it was. Young reported that in 1931 most people went by steam train[1] and 'suffered from overcrowding and several changes whilst journeying to their work. . . . The time spent—it took an hour and a quarter for a ten-mile journey with one change, and a third of the workers of Becontree had a longer journey than that in 1931, whilst others had more time-wasting changes—must have seriously depleted the few hours of leisure.'[2] As another writer put it, 'The hundred thousand settlers in the new East London town of Becontree . . . depended until 1932 on a railway laid down when Becontree was a cowshed.'[3]

There were other grounds for complaint. Virtually no public halls or other meeting-places were provided. The

---

[1] A check by the L.C.C. in 1927 had similarly found that 84% of the workers living on the estate travelled to work by rail.
[2] Young, T., op. cit., p. 139.
[3] Sinclair, R., *Metropolitan Man*, p. 293.

people who lived in what was then Dagenham Parish had no maternity and child welfare services at all, and no library until 1930. There were also few shops at first. Until new pubs were built after 1928, there were too few pubs and too little room in them. 'The "Robin Hood",' said Young, 'was little more than a cottage and the "Royal Oak" was no larger, but perhaps more modern. Both were hopelessly inadequate for the needs of the Estate people.'[1]

The Dagenham of those days provided perhaps the most dramatic illustration in Britain of how shortsighted it was to build estates of this kind, in which the social needs of the new residents were largely neglected.[2] The estate's defects were certainly widely recognized, and the criticisms it excited strengthened the case for the post-war new towns and for 'social planning' in general. Stanley Baldwin, for instance, then a leading member of the 'National Government' and soon to become Prime Minister, wrote in his introduction to Terence Young's book in 1934:

> I cannot help hoping that the restriction of 'housing' to the provision of houses alone may be reconsidered. To provide no halls or other buildings in which people can meet seems a serious mistake, whatever be the reason in law or policy. On another point the experience of Becontree is likely to be quoted. Industry is now following housing into Essex. To bring this about has taken a long time and it would perhaps be hardly safe to regard it as a good precedent.[3]

Mass-Observation, referring to Dagenham in 1942, spoke of 'these huge new communities, inhabited almost entirely by working-class people, planted down by one local authority in another local authority's area with inadequate

---

[1] Young, T., op. cit., p. 44.

[2] It is only fair to the L.C.C.'s officers at that time to say that the faults were by no means entirely theirs. The original plans for the estate were extremely enlightened. (See the *Report* by the Architect and Director of Housing to the L.C.C.'s Housing (Building and Development) Sub-Committee, 25 February 1920). The fact was that the Council had neither the powers nor the money to build the sort of new town (as it virtually was) that its officers envisaged.

[3] Baldwin, S., Introduction to Young, T., op. cit., p. 11. Baldwin wrote in his capacity as Chairman of the Pilgrim Trust, which had financed Young's survey.

planning and forethought about the social problems that would inevitably arise'.[1]

There is no doubt that some of Dagenham's more obvious lessons have been learned; the new towns set out to provide, from the start, the employment, the shops and the full range of community services that Dagenham had lacked. The irony is that, despite the lesson, there have been the same kinds of delays in providing services, the same difficulties with transport, in many of the post-1945 estates,[2] and even, to some extent, in new towns.[3] In practice, in other words, the experiences of migrants to more recent settlements have, in some respects, not been all that different from those of the first residents at Dagenham—which suggests that to examine how Dagenham has developed during the past 40 years may have some wider relevance.

[1] Mass-Observation, op. cit., p. 35. For other criticisms, see e.g. Lloyd, T. A., *Planning in Town and Country*, pp. 56–58, and P.E.P., 'Town and Country Planning', p. 7.

[2] White says of the L.C.C. out-county estates, 'even in the large post-war schemes all the essential community services, shops, transport, schools, recreation and churches have fallen hopelessly behind the build-up of population'. White, L. E., *New Towns*, p. 66. Jennings, discussing post-1945 estates in Bristol, reports, 'delay in providing services such as shops, public houses and transport facilities . . . the difficulties experienced in the inter-war estates were present also in the post-war developing areas'. Jennings, H., op. cit., p. 122. Nicholson, though stressing that the social needs were more adequately recognized by 1945, and that estates since then have been 'better planned', reports that 'the provision of social services and amenities . . . was often sadly lacking or delayed'. Nicholson, J. H., *New Communities in Britain*, p. 146.

[3] See White, L. E., op. cit., p. 66 and pp. 88–90, and Nicholson, J. H., op. cit., p. 127 and p. 146.

II

PEOPLE AND THEIR JOBS

THIS chapter sets out to give an impression of the kind of people who now live at Dagenham, and, in doing so, to consider also whether two major criticisms of the estate in its early years are still valid. One is the charge that the estate was 'one class'—in other words, overwhelmingly working class; the other that it was a 'dormitory'. These criticisms, which were certainly justified at the beginning,[1] are commonly levelled at housing estates. Together they amount to the suggestion that the place is, in some senses, a 'distorted' or 'freak' community, not a 'proper town'; and a distinctive feature of the new towns is that they set out to avoid both these faults—by having 'socially balanced' populations and by providing local employment.

Both problems were particularly glaring at Dagenham, when it was so much criticized on planning grounds in the 1930s and 1940s. The first applied with special force because of the vastness of the estate—a 'one-class' community of 90,000 people (or over 100,000, as it was then) is obviously more of an oddity, more of an offence to those who value 'social balance', than is one with a population of 2,000.

How does Dagenham stand on this score today? The occupational class of men on the estate is shown in Table 1, which for comparison also includes the figures for Bethnal Green and the country as a whole.

---

[1] See, e.g., Young, T., op. cit.: 'The occupied population is uniformly working class . . .' (p. 84). He also explained that in the first years '. . . with very few exceptions all the workers in the population had to travel to and from London each day, for there were hardly any employed locally except in the building industry' (p. 44).

TABLE I

OCCUPATIONAL CLASS OF MEN IN
DAGENHAM, BETHNAL GREEN, AND ENGLAND AND WALES

	Dagenham (1958)	Bethnal Green (1955)	England and Wales (1951)
Professional and managerial	4%	6%	18%
Clerical and shop workers ..	7%	12%	8%
Skilled manual	49%	49%	44%
Semi-skilled manual ..	22%	11%	16%
Unskilled manual	18%	22%	14%
Total ..	100%	100%	100%

This is comparing the men in the Dagenham general sample
in 1958 with those in the 1955 general survey of Bethnal
Green, and with occupied and retired men of 20 and over in
England and Wales. (See *Census, 1951, Occupation Tables*, pp.
148–149.) The occupational classes are based upon those used
by the Registrar-General in analysing the 1951 Census. (See
Classification of Occupations, 1950.) 'Professional and managerial'
correspond to the Registrar-General's Social Classes I and II,
'Clerical and shop workers' to the non-manual workers (people
in Socio-Economic Groups 6 and 7) in Class III, 'Skilled
manual' to the remainder of Class III, and 'Semi-skilled' and
'Unskilled manual' to Classes IV and V respectively.

As the table shows, manual workers amount to 74% of
men in the country as a whole, 82% in Bethnal Green, and
89% in Dagenham. By this yardstick, the estate is at least
as 'working class' as the East End itself and indeed as
anywhere in the country. Of the 157 English and Welsh
'towns' with populations of 50,000 or more examined by
Moser and Scott in a recent study, Dagenham had in 1951
the lowest proportion of people in the Registrar-General's
top two social classes (7.7% compared with a median of
15.8%), and was among the lowest (152nd) on the compo-

site 'Social Class index' used by the authors.[1] Their figures refer to the Borough of Dagenham, not the estate. If they were calculated for the estate, using the information from our general survey in 1958, the proportion of people in the top two classes would be even smaller (4%, as shown in Table 1), and the estate would come lower, measured by the 'Social Class index', than any of the other 'towns' examined.

A person's job is, of course, only one possible criterion of his social class. Indeed, in the course of this book, one of the key questions is how far the people at Dagenham are what is thought of as 'working class' in other ways—in their social behaviour, in their attitudes, and so on. I shall also examine what social class people say they belong to. Nonetheless, as a method of distinguishing people on the estate, I propose to use occupation as the criterion—men and single women being identified according to their own jobs, married, widowed and divorced women according to their husbands'. Retired men have been classified by their job at 60. I describe as 'working class' the men with manual occupations and their wives; as 'white collar people' the minority of those with, or married to men with, non-manual jobs. In discussing people who live elsewhere—some of those who have moved off the estate, for instance—I shall use the broader term 'middle class' to apply to people with managerial or professional occupations.

Table 1 shows the immense predominance of the 'working class' on the estate. But it also indicates that they are by no means all semi-skilled or unskilled workers. Though there are bigger proportions of these than in the country as a whole, they are outnumbered by skilled people. The same point was made, in a different way, by Young in 1934: '. . . the people of the Becontree Estate are not what is generally termed "slum people" . . . most slum dwellers could not afford the rents and travelling expenses.'[2] And

[1] Moser, C. A., and Scott, W., *British Towns*, p. 34 and p. 118.
[2] Young, T., op. cit., p. 25.

another study, of 6,400 people rehoused at Dagenham or elsewhere by the L.C.C. in 1936–8, supported this; it showed that, although the bulk of new accommodation provided at that time was outside London, only '7½% of the slum dwellers moved to new out-County cottage estates'.[1] It would thus be a mistake to think of Dagenham, then or now, as overrun by a kind of *lumpen proletariat*. The range of men's jobs and industries is wide, but characteristic occupations are toolmaker, machine operator, bodybuilder or foundryman in the engineering or motor industries; plasterer, foreman, bricklayer or labourer in the building industry; telephone or television engineer; electrician; printer; lorry or bus driver; dock labourer; engine driver, signalman or platelayer on the railways.

Where people work

Now to the second major question posed earlier—where do the estate's residents work? First, many work at the large local factory of the Ford Motor Company, which is, for many people outside the district, almost synonymous with 'Dagenham'; 'When you tell them you're from Dagenham,' said one man, 'they just think of Ford's.'[2] Ford's is as much a colossus among industrial plants as the estate among housing schemes: it covers 600 acres on the banks of the Thames, a few hundred yards south of the estate itself, and employs 35,000 workers. It has its own jetty, its own power station, its own blast furnace, its own private roads, its own police force. But the firm does not dominate the estate; Dagenham is far from a 'company town'. Nor, to look at it the other way round, do more than a minority of Ford employees live on the estate. Contrary to what is widely believed, Ford's went to the district from Manchester in 1931, when most of the estate had been

---

[1] Holmes, A. R., *Investigation into Effects of Rehousing by the L.C.C.*, p. 6.
[2] 'To many people,' another informant complained, 'Dagenham is just a place where the Zephyrs roll off the assembly line to the ecstatic squeal of girl pipers.' (The last is a reference to the Dagenham Girl Pipers, a local institution for over 30 years.)

completed, and it did not at the time provide very much employment for the estate people. Just the same, it is now by far the biggest local employer. Of the employed men in the general sample, 20% worked for Ford's, as did 6% of the employed women. Since one in five of the men on the estate is a Ford worker, virtually everybody knows someone, among relatives or neighbours, who works there.

Many other people also work locally, as Table 2 shows. This is a big change from the early years. In the beginning, few worked in the locality; most of the rest travelled to and from London every day. Even after ten years, in 1931, two-thirds of the employed men still worked in the County of London. But in 1958 the proportion was less than a third. In 1931 just over a quarter worked in Dagenham, Barking or Ilford. In 1958 more than half did so. (In 1931, as now, more women worked locally than men.)

TABLE 2

PLACE OF WORK, ACCORDING TO SEX OF INFORMANT
(General sample—employed men and women)

	Men	*Women*	*Men and Women*
Boroughs of Dagenham, Ilford or Barking	52%	69%	56%
Elsewhere in Essex	13%	6%	12%
County of London	30%	24%	28%
Elsewhere	5%	1%	4%
Total % ..	100%	100%	100%
Number ..	394	172	566

Of course, nearly a third of the estate's workers still do make the daily journey towards the centre of the metropolis —shop assistants and typists to the City or West End, dockers to Poplar or Stepney, cabinet-makers and upholsterers to Bethnal Green or Shoreditch. And to say that many people now work 'in the district' is somewhat misleading, because the estate itself is an immense residential area, and only a handful actually work within its boundaries. But Dagenham is clearly much less of a 'dormitory' than it was earlier on; and it is less so, for instance, than the post-1945 estate of Greenleigh or the private suburb of Woodford.

Affinities with the East End

In people's occupations, and in the proportion who work locally, present-day Dagenham is something like the East End. The affinities, of course, do not end there. It was always intended that the bulk of the estate's residents should come from the East London boroughs inside the County of London, and a large proportion have done so. Young showed that, out of a sample of tenants who had arrived up to 1929, nearly a third were from the East End itself, many more than from any other district. By 1958 the proportion was even higher; excluding those born at Dagenham, nearly half the people in the general sample (48%) were East Enders in origin.[1] Another 21% were from other boroughs—like Bermondsey, Islington and Finsbury—in the County of London, and the remaining 31% from other parts of the country.

Thus, although the estate was built expressly for Londoners, nearly a third of those who moved there came from outside the County of London. The reason is that throughout the 1930s the L.C.C. had more vacancies at Dagenham than it could easily fill with people from the County alone. The explanation has been suggested earlier; it is that the very slum dwellers for whom new housing was most desperately needed were, largely for financial reasons, reluctant to move out to far-off estates like Dagenham. In other words, the estate did not fully succeed in meeting the needs it was intended to. The L.C.C. found willing tenants by

[1] The definition of 'East End' used in both calculations is the boroughs of Bethnal Green, Hackney, Poplar, Shoreditch and Stepney.

relaxing its tenancy rules, first to admit people who worked in the County of London even if they did not live there, and then applicants who neither lived nor worked in London.

A few families came from Manchester or South Wales when Ford's big works was opened in 1931, but over two-thirds of the non-Londoners who moved into the estate to take advantage of the vacant council houses were, understandably, people living in the boroughs—Leyton, West Ham, East Ham, Barking—which lay between the Lea Valley (marking the London County boundary) and the estate itself.[1] Many of the districts they came from—examples are Stratford, Plaistow, Manor Park, Canning Town and Silvertown— seem in their occupational make-up and social character to be much like the East End; they were, in fact, themselves largely recruited from there originally. The result of all this is that predominantly the estate has drawn families from the East End and from similar sorts of districts inside and outside the County of London.

The people of Dagenham are thus largely working class in their jobs, and most of them come from working-class districts in London. As one goes about the estate and talks to its residents one is constantly reminded of this fact. The interviewer is often invited into the home with a good-humoured tolerance reminiscent of Bethnal Green. And in their speech most people are still unmistakably cockneys, the local rhythms and idioms owing nothing either to rural Essex or to middle-class suburbia. In some superficial ways, at least, these are recognizably the same kind of people as live in the older districts.

[1] This can be seen from the diagram on p. vi.

III

STABILITY AND THE PLACE
OF RELATIVES

TWO distinctive features help to account for the character of social life in the 'traditional' working-class community. One is that its population is relatively 'settled', in the sense that a large proportion of residents have lived there for many years. Another is that most people have relatives—parents, grandparents, brothers and sisters, uncles and aunts—close at hand. The two are connected, of course—if young people stay on in the same district after they marry they are likely to have their parents, and possibly their married brothers and sisters, living nearby.

The question, since long residence and kinship between them are so crucial in the development of the old-style community, is how far this kind of thing has happened at Dagenham. It is best examined in two stages—first, to what extent is the population now a settled one; and second, what part do relatives play in people's lives?

A settled population?

Dagenham's population was certainly unstable at the beginning. 'In those days,' as one man put it, 'people were coming and going as fast as you could see.' In the first ten years, 30,000 people—a third of all those who had gone to the estate—moved away again. The proportion leaving each year ranged between 7% and 17% of the total number of tenancies; the annual average over the decade was 10%, and it was still around this figure in 1932 and 1933.[1]

[1] Young, T., op. cit., pp. 210–11 and p. 240.

It is very different today. From 1956 to 1960 the removals amounted to only about 1% each year. These figures, for both the earlier and later periods, exclude families moving, by arrangement with the L.C.C., to other estates, new towns and so on. But when these are included for 1956–60, the total removals off the estate still amounted to less than 3% each year.

It looks as if Dagenham has turned right round in this respect. At the beginning, a great many people left the place; now comparatively few do so. The relative stability of the present population was reflected in the replies people gave when they were asked how long they expected to live on the estate. Of the 50 couples in the marriage sample, only four were actually seeking a move to another district, and in another six husband or wife or both were considering the possibility of moving away. The rest were content to stay and some were very anxious to do so.

'We expect to remain here for the rest of our lives. We like Dagenham and we don't want to leave it. We're acclimatized now and as far as I'm concerned we can go on living here for ever.'

'To tell you the truth, I hope my husband doesn't win the football pools, because if he did I suppose we'd have to buy a house and move away. I wouldn't like that. I said to him the other day, I said, "I'm settled here, I'm contented, I've got good neighbours. I don't ever want to go away from here." '

From what has already been said, it will be clear that, though the majority of tenants are now content to stay at Dagenham, there have, during the estate's history, been many changes in its population. Many people have left and their places been taken by others. What has been the net effect of all this, in terms of the length of residence of the present population? The dates when people arrived on the estate are given in Table 3.[1]

[1] The date of arrival is analysed according to informants' ages in Table 18, in Appendix 2.

TABLE 3

DATE OF ARRIVAL ON THE DAGENHAM ESTATE

Born on the estate		5%
Went to estate up to and including 1930 ..		25%
Went 1931–1939		38%
Went 1940–1945		12%
Went 1946 or later		20%
	Total % ..	100%
	Number ..	875

The number of people in this table is less than the total of 877 in the general sample because information about date of arrival was incomplete for two people. People are excluded for similar reasons from some later tables.

As this table shows, a quarter of the present residents are people who went to Dagenham in its first ten years. This may not, at first glance, seem very high. But if one compares Dagenham with other districts, it becomes clear that a relatively large proportion of the population are residents of long standing. A total of 68% of the people in the general sample were born at Dagenham or have been there since 1939 or before. The proportion who had lived in Bethnal Green for a similar period was 74%, in Woodford 48%. In other words, Dagenham's population is now very nearly as settled, measured in this way, as that of the East End borough, and much more so than the private suburb. To express it differently: in 1940 nobody had lived on the estate for 20 years; now over two-thirds of the adults have.

The estate's age structure

What has happened is that the estate has evolved from a new community, with a high turnover, to an older and more stable one. The effects of time can also be seen in the age distribution of the population. One of the characteristic problems of any new settlement is that its population is

22

'unbalanced' in age;[1] it is made up overwhelmingly of couples with young children—these being the kind of people most likely to need a home and most prepared to move to a new district to get one. 'In the main,' Terence Young said of Dagenham in the early 1930s, 'the population consists of married couples of ages from 30–45 with children under school-leaving age.'[2] There were very few middle-aged or old people.

There has been a big change since then, as Table 4 shows. The ages of people in the country as a whole in 1958 have been included for comparison.

TABLE 4

AGE DISTRIBUTION OF POPULATION
ON THE DAGENHAM ESTATE, 1931 AND 1958,
AND IN ENGLAND AND WALES, 1958

Age				Dagenham, 1931	Dagenham, 1958	England and Wales, 1958
0–4	..	..	..	15%	4%	8%
5–14*	..	..	..	29%	16%	15%
15†–29	..	..	..	19%	20%	19%
30–39	..	..	..	21%	13%	14%
40–49	..	..	..	11%	14%	14%
50–59	..	..	..	3%	17%	13%
60–69 ⎫					12%	9%
70 and over ⎭	..	..		2%	4%	8%
Total				100%	100%	100%

* 13 for Dagenham, 1931.
† 14 for Dagenham, 1931.

Sources: Dagenham, 1931—calculation from Young, T., op. cit., pp. 322–3. Dagenham, 1958—calculation based upon the membership of households of people in the general survey. England and Wales, 1958—*Annual Abstract of Statistics*, 1961, Table 9.

[1] See Williams, N., *Population Problems of New Estates*.
[2] Young, T., op. cit., p. 84.

The table suggests that there were still, in 1958, some important differences between Dagenham's age structure and that of the country generally—it looks as though the estate had less children under five and more people in their fifties and sixties. There were not, despite the impression of some Dagenham officials at that time, more people over 70, but there is no doubt that the numbers of old people are increasing rapidly, as the young married couples who went in the 1920s and 1930s move into their sixties and seventies. During the next 20 years the estate will have a larger proportion of old people than most districts. Dagenham is, in other words, still suffering from the lack of balance in its population during the first years. But it is much closer to a 'normal' age structure than it was.

Do parents live near?

Measured in these three ways—the proportion of tenants who now move away each year, the length of residence and the age distribution of the present population—it seems that Dagenham has largely overcome its early instabilities. Most people have lived there for a long time. One would think, on the face of it, that many also have relatives on the estate. Do they? And if they do, what patterns of relationships have evolved?

The key link between relatives, as the studies in the older districts have shown, is that between parents and their married children, and I propose to concentrate upon this relationship, beginning by looking at it from the viewpoint of young couples at Dagenham. Do many of the married people whose parents are alive have them living near? The answer is given in Table 5, which compares with Bethnal Green. Here, as elsewhere, 'married people' includes widowed and divorced.

In interpreting Table 5 one needs to take into account the difference between the two districts—Dagenham has twice the population of Bethnal Green and three times the area. Though nearly half the married people at Dagenham do have parents on the estate, it is clear that, apart from people actually

TABLE 5

PROXIMITY OF PARENTS—DAGENHAM COMPARED WITH
BETHNAL GREEN

(General sample—married people with at least
one parent alive)

Parents' Residence	*Dagenham*	*Bethnal Green*
Same dwelling	17% ⎫	12% ⎫
Within five minutes' walk ..	15% ⎬44%	29% ⎬54%
Elsewhere in the same district*	12% ⎭	13% ⎭
Adjacent district†	5%	17%
Further away	51%	29%
Total % ..	100%	100%
Number ..	332	369

* Dagenham—the estate: Bethnal Green—the same borough.
† Dagenham—those parts of the borough of Dagenham, Ilford and Barking which
are not on the estate; Bethnal Green—the rest of the 'East End', i.e. Hackney,
Stepney, Shoreditch, Poplar.

living *with* their parents, they live farther away from them
than do the married people of Bethnal Green. It will be
noted, in particular, that very few people on the estate have
parents living in other districts nearby. In Bethnal Green,
one could say, people's parents are often very near, but many
of those who are not are living within two or three miles.
At Dagenham, in the main, the parents who do not live on
the estate live away from it altogether.

The reasons for this contrast lie in the history of the
estate and in the way it has recruited its population. The
husbands and wives whose parents are on the estate are by
and large the people who have grown up there; their
parents, who were among the earlier tenants, now have these
married children living at Dagenham. The other married
people on the estate are mainly the more recent immigrants;
and they have left their parents behind in their old district—

a majority of the parents not on the estate live, in fact, in the East End or the inner Essex boroughs, the places from which so many of Dagenham's tenants have come. One can thus distinguish two broad groups among the younger couples. One is the husbands and wives who were born on the estate or brought up there. The other is those who moved to the estate after their marriage. Of course, such a distinction could be made in any district, but it is a particularly important one to make at Dagenham if one is to understand kinship patterns there.

Let me first look at the second group of people—the married men and women who have parents living, and who have moved to the estate since they married. They amounted to nearly two-thirds of the 332 married people in the Dagenham general sample whose parents are alive. They naturally included some people who moved to the estate in the late 1930s or during the war, but nearly half of them had gone since 1945.

As one would expect, comparatively few of these people had relatives on the estate. A quarter had parents there, and a quarter, similarly, had brothers and sisters. As was made abundantly clear in what people told us themselves, they are relatively isolated from their kin. And in what they said, particularly those who had arrived in the past decade, they often reproduced exactly the remarks of the migrants to new estates like Greenleigh.

Mr. and Mrs. Hunter, for instance, had moved to Dagenham from Bow in 1953:

'We were living in two rooms at the top of the house,' said Mrs. Hunter. 'We had our names down with the L.C.C. and they offered us this place, so we took it.' Mr. Hunter's parents, and most of his brothers and sisters, still live in Bow. So does Mrs. Hunter's mother, a widow, and her only sister—her three brothers have moved out of the East End, though not to Dagenham. 'We try to go up on a Saturday about once a month,' said Mrs. Hunter. 'We go to see his parents and then go on to my mother's place. We see the relatives a bit more in the summer,' she added, 'because they come down here to see us sometimes then.'

Others who had not been long at Dagenham explained how their contacts with relatives had been reduced by the move. 'We don't see each other anything like as much as we did in Shoreditch,' said Mrs. Steel. 'There we all lived opposite each other in the same street and we were always in and out of each other's homes. It's all different now—just an occasional meeting.'

Some obviously missed the aid of relatives, just like families on new estates.

'I was ill a few weeks ago,' said Mrs. Simpson. 'I had to stay in bed during the day and get up and manage somehow when the children came in from school. It's not like up there, where you've got someone to help you—you could always go to a sister or sister-in-law if you wanted anything. That's what you miss most.'

Such comments, as I say, echo those of couples at Greenleigh. But at Dagenham, even amongst those who went there after they married, there are some people with relatives—more than on the newer estate. This is because, particularly among those who moved before the war, relatives sometimes followed in each other's footsteps. 'One part of the family comes,' said Mr. Bedford, 'and the others follow. Take our case. My parents came from Stepney in 1937, then one of my sisters came with her husband, then the wife and I and then another brother. Eventually we were nearly all here.' One of the older tenants, Mrs. Gale, said, 'We came in 1929. My mother and father were dead and I didn't like leaving my sisters, but two of my sisters and one of my brothers followed me here. There were lots of houses empty then—you could easily get places here.'

Because tenancies have been less easy to acquire since 1945, this kind of collective migration has been more rare. But a few post-war immigrants also have relatives at Dagenham. Mrs. Hodgson, who moved to Dagenham from Islington in 1948, has her parents living in the next street. They were rehoused in a new council flat in Islington when their old home was demolished and were then able to arrange an exchange with a young couple who wanted to return to London. Most of the new-comers, however, do not have parents or other relatives near. In their day-to-day lives, like the people of Greenleigh or any other new settlement, they are cut off from their kin.

The extended families of Dagenham

Not so the people brought up at Dagenham. Again there are, of course, some exceptions. Mrs. Barton, for instance, was born on the estate, but her mother no longer lives there —she moved away to live with another daughter when the father died four years ago. Mrs. Carson moved to Dagenham from Bermondsey with her parents in 1931 and though her mother, now a widow, still lives on the estate, she is seldom seen. 'My father had T.B.,' Mrs. Carson explained, 'and I was sent away from home a lot. I was brought up mostly by an aunt—she's dead now—so Mum and I have never been all that close. She's got her own friends and she's mostly with them.'

But the great majority—four-fifths—of the married men and women in the general sample who grew up on the estate and whose parents are alive have them living there. Though, of course, these members of Dagenham's second generation are not necessarily married to other people who grew up locally, as many as two-thirds of them are.[1] There has been, in other words, a good deal of intermarriage between the younger people who have stayed on the estate, so that many have parents on both sides there. Of the 156 men and women in the general sample who were born or brought up at Dagenham, 140 had at least one parent or parent-in-law living. Of these 140 people, over nine-tenths had either parents or parents-in-law on the estate; over a third had both. These husbands and wives also see their parents often.

[1] Compare another 'second-generation' estate—at Sheffield. 'From the parish church register it was found that two-thirds of the inhabitants of the estate marrying there during the years 1927–1952 did in fact marry another resident.' Mitchell, G. D., *et al.*, op. cit., p. 90.

Among the women, for example, who had mothers living on the estate but not in the same house, over half had seen them during the previous 24 hours, and altogether nine-tenths had seen them at least once in the previous week. Among those living within five minutes' walk of their mothers, over two-thirds had seen them during the previous 24 hours.

The locally reared people often have other relatives at hand as well. Two-thirds had at least one brother or sister on the estate, and more than half of these had seen one or more during the previous 24 hours, another third at some other time in the previous week. Altogether, many of these members of Dagenham's second generation belong to local family groups—'extended families'—like those of the 'traditional' communities.

Mrs. Rank provides an illustration. She is now 34 and was born on the estate—her parents had moved from Stepney in 1922. The parents live 'just round the corner' and her two married sisters also live nearby.

> 'I see Mum pretty well every day,' Mrs. Rank explained. 'It's on the way to the shops, so I usually call in there to have a cup of tea and see if she wants anything. I sometimes call in on my sisters or I see them out shopping, but mostly I see them round at Mum's.' Mr. Rank remarked, 'We've got the wife's family living nearby. If she needs anything, if she's ill or anything like that, her mother or one of her sisters will always give her a hand.'

Other wives were similarly placed. 'My mother lives just in the next turning. I usually go round there every day to see her—to have a cup of tea and perhaps go out to the shops with her, and that sort of thing.' 'I go to mother's nearly every day—say about five times a week.'

People also spoke of the kind of regular help relatives gave each other. 'My mother,' said one wife, 'comes round every day to see me. She usually looks after the children while I go and do some shopping.' 'I go out to work,' said another, 'and my sister looks after the baby. My husband takes him round there in the morning and I collect him on the way back from work.'

Those with relatives close at hand on the estate described the part they played in their social life as well. 'On Saturday nights,' Mrs. Stansfield said, 'we go round to Mum's with the children. The men go out for a drink and we stay in and have a natter or look at the telly.' 'We've got a big family near here,' said Mrs. Potter. 'Most of our time is spent with relatives. We're always together—we even go away for holidays together.'

I have said that the extended families of Dagenham are like those of the older districts like Bethnal Green. The tie between mother and daughter, in particular, is again the axis of the family system. As much has been suggested in the examples quoted, and the figures confirm this impression. There is, for example, the usual tendency towards 'matri-locality' at Dagenham, in other words couples live with or near the wife's parents more often than the husband's. In the proportions of parents living on the estate as a whole, there is not a sharp difference—of the women in the general sample with parents alive, 48% have them at Dagenham; of the men 42%. But among those whose parents do live on the estate there are bigger variations, as Table 6 indicates.

TABLE 6

PARENTS' RESIDENCE AT DAGENHAM,
ACCORDING TO SEX OF INFORMANT

(General sample—married people with
parents living at Dagenham)

	Men	Women
Same dwelling	35%	40%
Within five minutes' walk ..	28%	40%
Elsewhere on estate	37%	20%
Total	100%	100%
Number ..	68	72

'Matrilocality' is almost as marked at Dagenham as in the
East End. How has it come about? Before 1945, when there
were usually more empty houses than prospective tenants,
daughters or sons who married could more or less choose
their house out of those vacant on the estate, near their
parental home or at a distance from it. 'I lived just round the
corner with my parents before we got married,' said Mrs.
Jarvis. 'In those days it was easy. Quite often you could get a
house in the same road, but if not you could be sure of find-
ing one in one of the streets nearby.'

That was in 1937. It is not the same today. But, even now,
mothers and daughters can arrange exchanges which bring
them closer to each other.

'We had our names down,' said Mrs. Barber, who lives in the
next road to her mother, 'and our first place was over by the
"Robin Hood". We had always lived over this way till then,
and I didn't know anybody over there. Mum kept looking
for an exchange for us, and as soon as she heard the people
here wanted a two-bedroomed house, instead of this three-
bedroomed one, she asked them if they'd exchange with us.
When they said they were willing she spoke to the rent
collector and it was all arranged.'

Two of Mrs. Payne's daughters lived in adjacent houses
opposite to her own.

'The eldest girl got the house over the way before the war;
you were given preference for your own children then of the
places that were going—then there were more empty. The
younger one couldn't get a place near here at first. She got a
house near Winchester Lane, but she got a transfer. My other
daughter knew the person next door was going, you see, so
she put in for it. Now we're all three near each other and it's
very nice and handy.'

The London County Council is, in fact, willing to help relatives to live near each other if they wish, by allowing
exchanges of this kind.

Note the contrast with the arrangements for allocating

tenancies in privately rented property in the older districts.[1] There, mothers can actually acquire tenancies for their daughters by 'speaking for' them to the rent collector. With the council property at Dagenham, as long as the demand exceeds the supply, the allocation of a council tenancy has to be determined on more 'objective' grounds. The personal influence of a mother with the local officials cannot get her daughter a council house. But once the daughter has been allocated a council tenancy, the familiar 'speaking for' system can then come into play, enabling the two to live nearer each other if they want to. And, plainly, they often do. Even under municipal management, the preference for couples to live near the wife's parents rather than the husband's is clearly and successfully expressed.[2]

In all sorts of other ways relationships with kin follow familiar patterns. Women see their mothers, and their fathers, more than men do. Of the 48 married women in the general sample who were born or brought up at Dagenham and whose mother is alive, 69% had seen her in the previous day; of the 60 men, 47%. And men, being drawn into their wives' extended families, see their mothers-in-law much more than women see theirs. Of the 62 married men in the general sample who were born or brought up at Dagenham and whose mother-in-law is alive, 44% had seen her in the previous day; of the 52 women, 19%.

The mother's home, again, is the most common centre for her daughters. 'Mother's is the general meeting-place,' said one wife, and another remarked, 'We all more or less gather round at Mum's.' Excluding those living with their parents, two-thirds of the married people's last contacts with their mothers had been at the parents' home, and the proportion

---

[1] See *Family and Kinship in East London*, pp. 24–27.

[2] I say 'even under' because there can obviously be conflicts between the needs of an efficient and 'just' administrative machine and those of relatives. As Jennings says in her study of municipal rehousing in Bristol: 'In the sphere of housing allocation . . . it was inevitable that some of the new Corporation tenants should contrast the workings of the vast, centralized machine with the days when they had only to "get in first" with a well-known landlord to bespeak a particular house.' Jennings, H., op. cit., p. 87.

was higher—over three-quarters—for those whose mother actually lived on the estate.

As in districts like Bethnal Green, husbands with parents on the estate regard it their duty to call on them regularly each week or fortnight—usually without their wife. 'My parents live near the "Fiddlers",' said Mr. Croom. 'I make a point of taking the kiddies over to see my mother every Sunday morning regular.' 'I try to see my parents once a fortnight,' Mr. Stansfield said. 'I missed this week, although it was really time for me to go, but that was so I could go next Sunday—it's Mother's Day, you see.'

The problem of the parents

In one way and another the husbands and wives who have grown up on the estate seem to be members of family networks like those of the East End. I now want to change the angle of vision and look at kinship from the viewpoint of the older generation at Dagenham. There was no special survey of old people, but the interviews with the 20 members of the tenants' sample—all of whom had married children alive—provide some illustrations to supplement the figures from the general sample.

First, just as some of the younger couples at Dagenham belong to extended families like those in the East End, so inevitably do some parents. Mrs. Millwood, who is as plump and talkative as an East End 'Mum', has much the same kind of life—a life in which her daughter and grandchildren play a central part.

'My daughter Vera lives just round the corner,' she said. 'She's in and out of here every day. So are the grandchildren. Brenda always calls in here on her way from school. She knocks on the door, and says "Is Mum here?" and goes straight to the toilet. She won't use the school's.'

Mr. Buckman is another who lives in the thick of his relatives. His daughter lives in the same road.

'She's always with her mother,' Mr. Buckman said. 'They go to the shops together, and Shirley watches the television with us round here of an evening. The grandchildren come and go as they like, and we give eye to them whenever it's necessary. I see a lot of my son-in-law, too—at the moment I'm helping him to build a garage next to his house for their little car.'

Other parents are more cut off. Mr. Travers, aged 68 and a chronic invalid, is one.

'It's my chest,' he said. 'It gets worse and worse every winter. I can't get out much. I have to stay here at home all day. We don't live here, we just exist.' His wife goes out to work. 'We couldn't manage otherwise.' They have four children, none of whom live on the estate—one is at Harlow, another at Upminster, a third in Islington, and the fourth in Birmingham. 'The last one I saw,' said Mr. Travers, 'was Bertie. He came over to see us one Sunday about six weeks ago.'

Mrs. Shearman, a widow, lives alone. She has three daughters, all of whom are buying their own bungalows—one at Cheam, one 'outside Birmingham', one at Westcliff. 'The one at Cheam,' she said proudly, 'has got a greenhouse with glass right down to the ground.' She goes to stay with one or another of her daughters for a week sometimes, and occasionally they come to see her. The last visit was three weeks before the interview. Mrs. Shearman seldom goes out; she spends her time knitting, listening to the radio or writing to her daughters, on cold days toasting her bunions by the single bar of the electric fire.

These are only isolated examples, and the question to be answered with the help of the general survey is how many people's circumstances are somewhat like those of Mrs. Millwood and Mr. Buckman, how many like those of Mr. Travers and Mrs. Shearman. The findings about the younger people would seem to suggest a clear conclusion. They divide into those who grew up on the estate and those who left their parents elsewhere to move to it, and since many of the former group have parents nearby, it would seem likely that many of the older generation have married children on the estate. But do they? The answer is given in Table 7, which again compares with Bethnal Green.

TABLE 7

PROXIMITY OF NEAREST MARRIED CHILD—
DAGENHAM COMPARED WITH BETHNAL GREEN

(General sample—people with at least one married child)

Residence of married child	Dagenham	Bethnal Green
Same dwelling	16%	23%
Within five minutes' walk.. ..	15%	27%
Elsewhere in same district* ..	14%	9%
Not in same district	55%	41%
Total %	100%	100%
Number	369	277

* Dagenham—the estate; Bethnal Green—the same borough.

Table 7 shows that over half the parents at Dagenham with a married child do not have one living on the estate, and that, in general, they do not have sons and daughters as near as their counterparts in the East End borough. The variation is reflected in contacts with children; 58% of the Bethnal Green people with married children had seen one in the previous 24 hours, compared with 45% of those in Dagenham.

How can these findings be reconciled with what has so far been reported? The younger people who have grown up at Dagenham and now live there have parents on the estate, but many fewer of the older generation have children there. What is the explanation? It is not that the parents, like so many of the younger people discussed earlier in the chapter, are relative new-comers to Dagenham; over nine-tenths of the people on the estate aged 50 and over have lived there since before 1946. It is clear, therefore, that what has happened is that many sons and daughters who grew up on the estate have since moved away from it and from their parents. But left unanswered is the question of why they have gone.

This chapter thus presents some paradoxes. The patterns of kinship relationships at Dagenham are in many ways like those to be found in the older working-class communities—young couples living with or near their parents, mothers 'speaking for' their daughters with rent collectors, daughters clustering near their mothers, and so forth. In its essentials, this is clearly the same kinship system, transplanted from the bustling streets of the East End to the flat, open landscape of the Thames Estuary. Time has, to a large extent, restored the patterns of the past. But all this applies only to some people on the estate, not to all, and the exceptions are of two main kinds—the young people who have moved in from London, and the parents whose children have all moved away from the estate. The movement of the two sets of younger people—those coming to Dagenham, and those leaving it—is, in fact, part of the same process. How this works, and the ways it has affected Dagenham's development, are examined in the next two chapters.

IV

PRESSURES ON THE SECOND GENERATION

WHY have so many members of Dagenham's second generation moved away? There are a number of reasons. The first is that there has been a big increase in the numbers of people wanting houses on the estate. As was noted in the last chapter, Dagenham had an unbalanced age structure to start with; it was overwhelmingly populated by couples with young children. But most of the estate had been built up by the early 1930s, and little room was left to allow for the 'natural increase' of population—the 'bulge' in the demand for local homes that would inevitably come when the children of the first tenants grew up and married.

The biggest part of the first generation to be brought up on the estate was born between about 1920 and 1935, and would have reached the age of 25 between about 1945 and 1960. Since children under 14 amounted to nearly half the population of the estate in the early 1930s, a big expansion in housing demand was inevitable. An estate with the age structure that Dagenham had in 1931 would, after 30 years, need an automatic increase of something like a third in its houses to meet this natural increase, assuming that there was no net movement of population in or out and that the birth-rate had been much the same as in the country generally.[1]

---

[1] This conclusion, based upon our own calculations, seems to be confirmed by the L.C.C.'s team that drew up plans for a new town at Hook in Hampshire. Though the proposal was dropped in 1960, the team's work has been published in *The Planning of a New Town*. Figure 9, p. 19, in that report shows the projected changes in population over the first 75 years in the life of a new town with an 'unbalanced immigrant population'.

The need to prepare for this kind of population growth is something that the post-war new towns have come to recognize, though most did not anticipate it early enough. The solution at Dagenham would have been either to have built a smaller estate to begin with, leaving land for expansion later, or to have built as large an estate, but to have reserved substantial sites nearby. Some new houses have been built locally—about 600 have been provided since 1945 by the L.C.C. on the 'Heath Park Extension' to the estate, and the Dagenham Borough Council itself has built about 4,000 houses in its borough, most of which have been occupied by the sons and daughters of L.C.C. estate tenants. Barking and Ilford have also, to a smaller extent, done the same. But the new houses that have been built nearby, publicly or privately, since the estate was completed, have not been enough to meet the needs, and there is now virtually no more land available. Dagenham Council still had, in March 1962, a housing waiting list of 1,700, of whom over half were the married children of L.C.C. tenants, as were over a quarter of the 2,000 families on Barking Council's list at the same date.

Ironically, in an attempt to meet the need, Dagenham Borough Council has had to provide 'overspill' housing of its own—at Canvey Island, another 20 miles to the east. One husband remarked bitterly about this, 'It's a ridiculous situation. The L.C.C. puts its overflow into Dagenham. Dagenham puts its overflow, of necessity, out to Canvey Island. Where they go from Canvey Island in the next generation, God knows. We can only assume they'll put them on rafts and set them adrift.'

No small homes

Dagenham's problem is aggravated by the lack of diversity in the size of its dwellings, which are overwhelmingly two- and three-bedroomed. The more variety there is in the sizes of homes in a district, the easier it is for people to

38

change house without leaving the locality.[1] Only 4% of the dwellings on the estate are of one or two rooms;[2] in Bethnal Green, at the time of the 1951 Census, 21% of the dwellings were of this size.[3] Because Dagenham has so few small dwellings, the result is that, though some houses are crammed tight with two families, others are too large for parents whose children have now left home. Judged by the L.C.C.'s own standards of accommodation, about a tenth of the dwellings on the estate are overcrowded and no less than half under-occupied.[4] As many as 42% of the people over 60 in the general sample lived alone or just with their husband or wife—the great majority of them in two- or three-bedroomed houses.

The L.C.C. does what it can to ease this problem by transferring people into more appropriate-sized homes that fall vacant and by arranging exchanges between those whose homes are too large or too small; nearly 600 families each year switched in these two ways in 1959 and 1960 to other dwellings on the estate. But these movements were all voluntary. The L.C.C. takes the view, rightly, that it would be wrong to try to force people out of houses that are 'too large' for them, even though the housing problem would obviously be eased if this were done. There are, in any case, obvious limits to what could be achieved by mutual exchanges within the Dagenham estate itself, because of the shortage of small homes there.

There are all sorts of reasons why old people may be reluctant to move to smaller homes, even if they are available. One is attachment to the house or the garden. 'We've been in this house thirty-three years,' said Mr. Shephard,

---

[1] This point was made in an earlier study of Bethnal Green. 'Like most long-established communities, Bethnal Green has diverse dwelling types and internal mobility is thus made possible. The fact that there is such a high incidence of internal mobility inside Bethnal Green is a testimony of people's attachment to the borough. The diversity of local dwelling types, in turn, facilitates the growth of such attachments.' Glass, R., 'Social Aspects of Town and Country Planning', p. 214.
[2] L.C.C., *London Housing Statistics, 1958-1959*, p. 41 and p. 52.
[3] *Census 1951, London*, p. 15.
[4] These standards are reproduced in Appendix 3.

'We're used to it. I've got my tool shed out there—I wouldn't like to give that up, or the garden I've put so much work into.' Another is the wish to keep extra rooms so that relatives can stay, all the more necessary when children have moved away to other districts. 'I know I've got spare bedrooms up there,' said Mr. Gale, 'but them spare bedrooms are very handy if any of the children or grand-children want to stay the night.' A third deterrent is expense —the rent of a new smaller flat may be as high as that of an older house, and there is also the cost of moving.[1]

But though many older people are reluctant to move,[2] some would do so if smaller dwellings were offered nearby. Mrs. Payne was one.

> 'I've got two bedrooms doing nothing,' she said. 'I say to Dad sometimes I hardly think it fair that we should have a house like this when other people have got families. But then, on the other hand, to get a smaller place we'd have to move away from here. I've got my daughters living opposite, and I'm never without one of them. I'd miss them, you see, and then I'd have to make a lot of new friends.'

Plainly, had Dagenham been provided with more small dwellings, mixed up with the large, some parents like Mr. and Mrs. Payne would have moved into them and released larger houses for growing families. As it is, not only has the estate too few dwellings for its expanded population; many of those it has are not putting their precious space to full use.

---

[1] The L.C.C. is prepared to pay removal expenses up to a maximum of £25. But, generous though this may seem, people are still deterred by expense. Mr. Travers said, 'There's always extra expense if you uproot yourself. You need new lino, new curtains, and that sort of thing.'

[2] The relative immobility of older people was illustrated in a recent national survey, which showed that, though 'older small households' accounted for 22% of all households, they formed only 11% of those who had moved in the previous 12 months. Donnison, D. V., Cockburn, C., and Corlett, T., *Housing Since the Rent Act*, p. 80. Old people's attitudes towards moving were explored in a small survey into the demand for old people's dwellings in a South Devon parish. See Willmott, P., and Barbour, P., 'Housing of Old People in a Rural Parish', pp. 159-61.

L.C.C. policy on tenancies

These are not the only obstacles to married children who want to stay on the estate. Few houses, as I have shown, are available. But the bulk of the homes that do fall vacant are denied to the people who have grown up at Dagenham. The reason is that the L.C.C. has continued to reserve most of the vacated houses for rehousing new-comers from London. Something like 300 of the 27,000 houses on the estate fall vacant each year. Of these, 100 are allocated to Dagenham and Barking Borough Councils (68 to the former, 32 to the latter) for the 'sons and daughters of tenants'. Sons and daughters who have married and have continued to live with their parents can also sometimes take over the tenancy when the parents die—about 100 tenancies are transferred in this way annually. But every year about 200 vacant houses on the estate go to new immigrants from London—mostly young couples. As many as 42% of the people now in their thirties who live on the estate have arrived since 1945.[1] Thus while young married people move into Dagenham from the older London districts under the L.C.C.'s aegis, many of the people who grew up on the estate—of similar ages to the immigrants—go off to live elsewhere. This is part of the explanation for the findings about kinship in the previous chapter; and it serves to qualify the suggestion made earlier in that chapter that the estate has now 'settled down'.

The L.C.C. has not always seemed so insensitive to the needs of local people. In the early 1930s, when there was still some difficulty in letting houses on the estate, it introduced the 'sons and daughters rule', under which the married children of tenants were eligible for houses on the estate. Mr. and Mrs. Grove found it easy enough in 1938:

> 'We both came down here with our families when we were children,' said Mrs. Grove. 'We got married in 1938, and we got this house within three weeks. We've lived here ever since.

[1] This can be seen from Table 18, in Appendix 2, which shows when people arrived on the estate, according to their age.

In those days you just told them you were married or were going to get married, and they came round with keys for lots of houses within a few days. You more or less had your choice.'

People said that it was like this until the end of the war in 1945. It became increasingly hard after that. For one thing, there was the general post-war demand for houses—so great was the pressure on the L.C.C. that it could easily have filled half a dozen Dagenhams. What is more, the estate's population 'bulge' was beginning to reach marriage age around that time, so that a specifically second-generation demand was building up at the same time as the general one. As a result of these pressures, the L.C.C. revoked the 'sons and daughters rule' in 1952, at first disclaiming any responsibility for the children,[1] and then agreeing to the annual quota of tenancies mentioned earlier. Because the demand was so great, many children who wanted houses at Dagenham could not get them even before the change in L.C.C. policy—they had to take their places in a long queue alongside Londoners who also wanted homes. But they probably did rather better than they have since; from figures made available to me by the L.C.C., it looks as if something between 250 and 300 'sons and daughters' each year got L.C.C. homes between 1945 and 1952, compared with the present quota of 100.[2]

The L.C.C.'s case for giving most of the vacancies on the estate to Londoners is a strong one. The estate, paid for out of London's rates, was created to help ease London's housing problem, and the County of London is still desperately short of homes. In 1956, 300,000 people—nearly a

---

[1] A L.C.C. spokesman, addressing the Royal Commission on Local Government in Greater London, argued that the responsibility for housing the sons and daughters properly lay with the local councils in the area: '. . . the family having moved to an out-County estate becomes a family with loyalties to a new area, not only loyalties, but paying rates to a new area; and it is therefore reasonable to look to that new area to make provision in so far as it can for the people housed within its area.' Royal Commission on Local Government in Greater London, *Minutes of Evidence*, 11-12, pp. 430-1. This is quoted in Cullingworth, J. B., *Housing in Greater London*, which briefly discusses 'the Becontree problem', p. 14.

[2] Some sons and daughters who were rehoused were given L.C.C. houses on the new estates, like Debden and Harold Hill, then being built further out in Essex.

tenth of the population of the County—were without a home of their own.[1] Naturally, the L.C.C. wants every one of the vacant tenancies it can get in out-County estates like Dagenham to help with this problem, and considers generous its allocation of an annual quota to local people. Some people at Dagenham themselves recognized its needs. 'There are families living in one room in London,' said one wife, 'and I think they need the houses more.' 'The houses should go to the most deserving cases,' a husband said. 'There's so much overcrowding in London that they should come first.'

Others thought differently. 'We made our way here,' said one. 'The children were born and bred down here, so they're surely entitled to a house. But they're still bringing people in from Poplar and places like that.' 'I think the L.C.C. should rehouse the sons and daughters at Dagenham, like they did before the war,' another argued. 'They've grown up here and they should come before Londoners. After all, it's those people and their families who've helped to build up the estate.' This is also the official view of the Dagenham and Barking Councils, who wish either to buy the L.C.C. houses in their boroughs, or at least to have control of all tenancies falling vacant.[2] And certainly if the 200 or so vacancies each year which at present go to new migrants from London had been available for the sons and daughters at Dagenham, this would obviously have been of some help. Over ten years, at least 2,000 more members of the second generation could have stayed on the estate.[3]

Another argument in favour of local control over tenancies has been put by Richardson, who carried out a case-study of the population and housing problems of Barking,

[1] *Administrative County of London Development Plan, First Review 1960, County Planning Report*, p. 25.
[2] See the Dagenham Borough Council's evidence to the Royal Commission on Local Government in Greater London, *Minutes of Evidence*, 16–17, pp. 610–12.
[3] I say 'at least 2,000' because, though some of the tenants would be married to people from other districts, many—in fact, something like two-thirds, if our general sample is a reliable guide—would have husbands or wives born or brought up on the estate, so that 2,000 tenancies might mean over 3,000 married sons and daughters rehoused.

as part of a wider inquiry in metropolitan Essex. He says:

> . . . the problem of the London County Council with very
> serious under-occupation by small and ageing households and
> no means of providing alternative accommodation for these
> people is one which cannot be resolved in present circum-
> stances. But, if reciprocal arrangements were to be made with
> Barking, the latter could build a much higher proportion of
> small dwellings in their redevelopment areas for people from
> Becontree, thereby freeing property on the L.C.C. estates to
> meet the demand from young families. If all the property
> owned by the London County Council and the local council
> [Barking] had been administered by a single Housing Authority,
> the advantages to be gained through greater flexibility would
> soon have been apparent.[1]

The argument applies with equal force to Dagenham Borough
Council. Local control of the estate would not only have
increased the number of vacant houses available for the
second generation. It could also have made it easier to use
more fully the houses in the area. But this has not been done.

Do people want to stay?

I have shown so far that there are influences at Dagenham
that make it difficult for married sons and daughters to stay.
But is it certain that they would have wanted to? In order
to get at the reasons why second-generation emigrants from
Dagenham have left, we asked the 20 parents in the tenant's
sample about those of their children who had moved. They
had 59 married children between them, of whom 42—
between two-thirds and three-quarters—had left Dagenham.
We asked the parents whether, as far as they could judge,
their children had wanted to go and if so why. I supplemented this with interviews with a few of the children
themselves, following a sample of 16 of those living in the
Greater London area or in Essex to their present home to
ask them for their own views. What the 16 said did not
necessarily always tally with what their parents had reported,

[1] Richardson, M., *Post-War Population and Housing Trends in Metropolitan Essex*,
pp. 65–66.

44

as might have been expected; but the conclusion that I would draw, from the interviews with members of both generations, is that, of the 42 children who now live off the estate, the proportion who would have preferred to stay there if they could was at least a third.

The numbers are obviously too small, and the evidence too hypothetical, to put much weight on this. But there is, it seems to me, more substantial evidence to support the view that, even though they may be a minority of all those who have gone, many sons and daughters have moved away from Dagenham unwillingly. Consider, for instance, Table 8, which shows the proportions of married children living on the estate, according to their age. Bethnal Green is included for comparison; in that district the older that people are, the more likely they are to have moved away from their parents—less sons and daughters aged 40 and over lived in the borough than of 39 and under. In Dagenham the opposite is true.

TABLE 8

PROPORTIONS OF MARRIED CHILDREN LIVING IN SAME
DISTRICT AS PARENTS, ACCORDING TO AGE OF CHILDREN
DAGENHAM COMPARED WITH BETHNAL GREEN
(Married children of people in general samples)

	Dagenham		*Bethnal Green*	
	Age of married children		Age of married children	
	39 and under	40 and over	39 and under	40 and over
Proportion of married children living in same district*	27%	44%	41%	31%
Total numbers of married children ..	797	126	504	213

* Dagenham—the estate; Bethnal Green—the borough.

This table suggests that many of the younger people have been frustrated from doing the same as their older fellows, and that, were houses as freely available as in the past, more of the children who grew up in Dagenham would live there still.

Other evidence supports the same conclusion. As many as 3,000 families, then on the Dagenham Borough Council's housing list, were told in 1954 that their names had been removed because the Council could offer them no hope of a home in the district, and it seems clear that a large proportion of these, together with many others, gave up waiting and moved elsewhere.

> 'My son tried for years to get a place here,' said Mrs. Gale. 'He had his name down for years and never got offered anything. He made up his mind the only way they'd ever get a house was if they bought it themselves. It was the same with my daughter. She was on the waiting list living here with us for years until they decided they didn't stand a chance and they'd have to move away from Dagenham.'

Another thing that suggests that there is a substantial demand for homes at Dagenham among the second generation is that so many share a home with their parents. More than a third of the married people in the general sample who had been born or brought up on the estate, and whose parents were still alive, were actually living *with* them. To look at it the other way round, a quarter of the people in the general sample who were 60 or over had married children living in the same home. And four-fifths of the couples sharing a house with parents were in homes where the parents were the tenants—in other words, most couples were living in their parents' homes rather than the other way round.

Some of those living with parents said they would not move to a home of their own if they had the opportunity to do so. Mr. Bradshaw lives with his wife's mother—the father had died three months before the interview. 'We were waiting for a place of our own,' he said, 'but now the old man's gone we couldn't leave the old lady on her own. We shall stay on here now—not that there's much chance of them offering us somewhere of our own.' Mr. and Mrs. Rust live with the husband's mother; the wife explained:

'We shouldn't leave his Mum on her own. I don't suppose you'd like to live on your own when you're old and can't do anything. And as for putting them in a home, well it's not fair. They've lived here for years and they've put their roots down, and it's not fair uprooting them, so we decided to stay here with her.'

But this is not, it seems from our interviews, the most common explanation for people sharing with parents. Most said they did so because this was the only way they could have a home in Dagenham, or perhaps a home at all.

The attractions of Dagenham

It is not possible even to estimate how many, but it seems certain that some thousands of people have moved away from the estate since 1945 who would have chosen to remain. There are a variety of reasons why they might have preferred to stay. The first and most obvious is the appeal of a house at a reasonable rent—to have been offered a house at all on the estate would inevitably have meant a council tenancy, something that many couples living in any district would have valued highly in recent years.

A second reason is attachment to the familiar locality. 'If you've grown up here,' said Mr. Wright, still in Dagenham, 'it's the place you're used to and naturally you want to go on living here.'

'I don't think I'd get on in another district,' said another man still on the estate. 'It's just the thought of leaving Dagenham. I mean I've been here all these years—we came from Hoxton when I was seven and I'm thirty-two now—and I like it here, and this is where I want to stay.'

Others, like Mr. Brooks, who lives with his wife's parents,

spoke also of his attachment to the other residents and to his job:

> 'They'd offered us a place further afield, they said we could go to Basildon or Harlow. But I don't want to go away from Dagenham. I like the district and I like the neighbours here. I work locally too; I don't want to have to change my job.'

Another reason some people gave for wanting to stay was their desire to stay near relatives. 'I like it here and I wouldn't want to move,' said Mrs. Stansfield, 'If I want anything I can always go round to Mum. I couldn't do that if I moved away. And I would miss her, I really would.' 'We were both born and bred in Dagenham,' Mrs. Rank explained, 'We've got relatives here and we like it here. It's nicer when you've got your family near.' Another wife, living with her parents, said:

> 'I would miss my mother and my sister if we moved away, but we're overcrowded here. I suppose we'll have to go to Debden or Basildon or somewhere like that, and start all over again, just like Mother had to thirty years ago.'

A daughter who had moved from Dagenham to the East End, explained:

> 'We'd have loved to have lived there. We'd have jumped at anything there, but we didn't stand a chance. The only place we could get was two rooms in Shoreditch, near where my husband worked. Two years later they pulled down the old house we were in and rehoused us in this flat [still in Shore-ditch]. It's very nice, we're quite happy really, except that we would have liked to have gone back home—with the family. I get a bit jealous here at times. I've got a friend across the road—Yvonne—she lives right near her mother. If anything goes wrong, you can go to your mother, and you can help her if she needs it. When you're like that you're a *family*— you're together, not all spread all over the shop like we are.'

The efforts of some other people to move back from other districts shows how strongly attached to Dagenham they were. There were again a number of reasons why people might want to transfer back to Dagenham—it might be for their work, or the familiarity of the district or the presence of former friends—but the relatives often seemed to figure among the reasons for returning. Mr. and Mrs. Knight's first home of their own was in the post-war L.C.C. estate at Harold Hill.

> 'We were living with the wife's mother in Walker's Gardens after I was demobbed. We were overcrowded there and I applied to be rehoused by the L.C.C. After about two years— it was in 1948—they told us we could have this place at Harold Hill. We stayed there for about two years, but the wife wanted to come back here. We put an advert. in the *Dagenham Post*, and got someone who wanted to transfer. The wife wanted to be near her mother and sisters. That was the main issue really. She didn't like Harold Hill because she didn't like being away from them.'

> 'When we got married,' said Mrs. Croom, 'we lived in Hackney, because we couldn't get a house. We tried and tried and we were on the list for a long time, but it was no good. Then we moved into a condemned flat in Bethnal Green because we heard that they were coming down. We got in there quick so that the L.C.C. would have to move us, and when they did we put down for Dagenham. We wanted to be here because we'd both been brought up here.'

Mr. and Mrs. Tomlinson's reasons for returning from Basildon were more complex.

> 'We came back partly because of my husband's work, and the other reason was because my mother was very ill,' said Mrs. Tomlinson. 'My sister had gone out to Pitsea and there was no one near. I got this house opposite her. I think it's better for both of you if you're near.'

The last chapter showed that some extended families like those of the East End have grown up in Dagenham. The present one has shown that, despite all the difficulties in getting houses on the estate, some people have made great efforts to get back to the district—and, in at least some instances, to reunite with their kin. As an article on 'Mum' said in a Dagenham journal, 'Rehouse her married daughter in a spanking new house complete with hot and cold running television, and if it's more than a threepenny ride from her mother she will begin a series of Machiavellian manoeuvres to exchange back nearer "home" even if it means taking sub-standard accommodation.'[1] A study of a Liverpool housing estate noted the same process: 'Considering the restrictions and difficulties,' said the authors, 'it is remarkable how many families have relatives on the estate', and they added that this was 'an indication of the great importance families attach to maintaining close ties with parents and parents-in-law.'[2]

Despite the success that some people at Dagenham have had, however, in changing houses so as to get back to the estate, there can be little doubt that there would be still more extended families on the estate, and fewer parents left alone, if all the sons and daughters who wanted to stay had been free to do so. If the estate had been planned to allow for the 'natural increase' in its population, and if all the vacancies were at the disposal of the second generation, in other words, Dagenham's patterns of kinship would even more closely resemble those of the older communities of the East End. More is involved, of course, than this. If all the married children who wanted to had been able to stay, Dagenham would have more of a settled population than it has now, and would be more of a 'stable community'. It would, in yet another way, be even more like Bethnal Green than it is.

[1] Cannon, L., 'Mum', *Dagenham Digest*, January 1961, p. 27.
[2] Mitchell, G. D., *et. al.*, op. cit., p. 62 and p. 74.

V

THE VOLUNTARY EMIGRANTS

THE previous chapter has dealt with only part of the
story of the second generation movement away from
Dagenham. It is clear that, apart from the planning
mistakes and the management policies which have forced
people off the estate, other kinds of pressures have also been
at work. Many—almost certainly the majority—of the
married sons and daughters who have moved away from
Dagenham actually chose to do so; they would not have
stayed even if they could. In this chapter I want to look at
their motives.

Among the 16 sons and daughters whom I followed to
their new address, there were eight who quite certainly
had gone from choice. From the interviews with them, and
with parents whose children had gone willingly, the various
reasons became apparent. Some moved to follow their job.
They had, for instance, managerial or professional occupations of the kind that demand geographical mobility. One of
Mrs. Lee's sons has migrated not only from the estate but
from the country; he is 'in Canada, managing a canning
factory. He wasn't content to go back and forward to the
same job every day. He wanted progress.' Mr. Bird's two
daughters live respectively in a Birmingham suburb and in
Chelmsford. 'One is married to a doctor, the other a teacher.
They have to be there for their husband's jobs.'

A new house, a new district

Others went because they wanted a better house than
those available in Dagenham. 'The houses back at Dagenham', one son explained, 'are not my ideal sort of home.

They don't have the kind of modern conveniences we expect these days.' Another said, 'This house is much bigger. At Dagenham the bedrooms are like rabbit hutches.' He had also wanted a bigger garden, and more privacy. 'There's the garden as well', he added, 'it's 100 feet long, about 32 feet wide, much bigger than anything in Dagenham. It's surrounded by a hedge. We've got a certain amount of privacy here that we would never have had if we'd stayed— there was just a chestnut fencing, and if you went into the garden you were on view 40 or 50 yards all round.'

Some had wanted to buy a house rather than rent one. 'My children never wanted to stay here,' Mrs. Hamilton explained, 'They wanted to buy their own houses.' Another man, whose three children had left Dagenham, said, 'They've had the option to better themselves, and they have bettered themselves by buying their own houses.'

Others again wanted to live in a different kind of district from Dagenham, a less uniform one perhaps or more architecturally distinguished. 'My brother Arthur,' said a son who has stayed in the district, 'used to fume against what he called the "little red boxes" of Dagenham, the lack of any outstanding architectural features, the formlessness. He wanted to get out.' 'When I was 18,' explained one of those who had gone, 'I really started formulating my ideas regarding living in the area that I wished to live. I was looking for somewhere away from the drabness. It was so stereotyped, the streets and the houses were all the same.' 'At Dagenham,' said another son, 'you look out of your house and you see rows and rows of council houses. You accept that as part of your life, but to me it got monotonous. Whereas now I can look down to the golf course at the bottom there and the bungalows opposite. It's a pleasant outlook front and back.'

Then there were others who wanted to live in a 'socially superior' neighbourhood; as one father put it, 'They wanted to aspire to a higher social plane.' Two mothers illustrated this sort of attitude when they explained what their children thought of Dagenham.

'Johnnie lives at Upminster,'[1] said one. 'He was dead against living here, no inclination to stay on the estate at all. When he was at home here with us, he never liked it. He said he always hated having that Dagenham address on his letters. He's a commercial traveller, you see.'

'We went and stayed with my son and daughter-in-law recently,' said the other, whose son is an insurance manager. 'My daughter-in-law said to us one day, "Of course, we wouldn't come to live at Dagenham in any circumstances." It's a matter of the estate, you see. They at Kingston have risen above Dagenham.'

Two daughters, now living in semi-detached houses in private suburbs, expressed their views like this:

'I certainly wouldn't live at Dagenham. Certainly not. It's perfectly awful. The class of people living there—without being snooty—they're a shocking class of people.'

'I don't like the place. It's not that we're snobs, but I find it a depressing place. After all, it's a slum clearance estate, isn't it?'

And two of the husbands who had also moved to private suburbs were concerned for their children rather than themselves:

'I think it's better for them. The children round here seem to be somehow—without being a prig—better spoken, better behaved, there's no East End accent or anything about them.'

'There's more scope for the children here. I'm not a snob by any means, but if you bring the children up with, shall we say,

---

[1] Upminster, a suburb of private estates four miles east of Dagenham, was mentioned by other informants. 'We have, in fact, a Dagenham colony at Upminster,' said one. Another, whose sister lived there, remarked, 'It's a big joke with us to call my sister and her husband the Duke and Duchess of Upminster. . . . Over there it's all big cars and big houses, and here it's all small cars and council houses.'

people with better income brackets, they tend to look for higher things in life.'[1]

It is not surprising to find attitudes of these kinds among some of the people who grew up at Dagenham. They are present in any district. Similar aspirations motivate people still leaving central districts in London for housing estates and new towns, and were evident among some of Dagenham's present residents. 'Coming to Dagenham from Bethnal Green,' said Mr. Williams, 'you felt you were moving into a superior area. You were taking a step up.' But, though Mr. Williams was content to stay at Dagenham, other tenants on the estate were not. Some of the people still living at Dagenham, in other words, expressed views similar to those of some of the sons and daughters who have already gone.

> 'It's where you live that counts most of all,' said one man, who works as a supervisor in a department store in nearby Ilford. 'If you live in Bethnal Green and Stepney and all those rough places you haven't got a chance, and it's not much better down here. Superior sorts of people live in places like Ilford. This estate's not doing me or the children any good, and the sooner we can get away the better.'

> 'A council estate is all right for some people,' said a clerk, 'but I think we can do better than that. What I want to do is to get a house or bungalow of my own out at Hockley or Rayleigh or somewhere like that.'

A television engineer living on the estate said that he wanted to 'move away to something better—to better ourselves if we possibly can'. The impression from the interviews with the marriage sample is that it is among white-collar people or highly skilled manual workers that one

---

[1] The reader may note that the same disclaimer—'I'm not a snob', etc.—occurs in all these four quotations from ex-Dagenham sons and daughters. This is not due to deliberate selection on my part; this was, in fact, a constant refrain. These people, who are all in some sense or another 'socially mobile', are obviously at one and the same time concerned about social class differences and sensitive about their very concern.

finds the Dagenham residents who are most anxious to leave the estate.

People who were middle class in occupation or in aspirations or taste also seem to bulk large among the married children who have moved off the estate—and especially those who went from choice. Those described by their parents or themselves as willing emigrants include, for instance, a doctor, teachers, scientists, business or factory managers, clerks; those who would have liked to stay are predominantly manual workers—an electrician, for instance, a docker, a semi-skilled factory worker. There also seem, if our small samples of parents and of emigré children are a reliable guide, two other differences between the voluntary and the reluctant leavers. The former more often own their own houses; the latter more often rent theirs. The former more often live in suburban or semi-rural districts; more of the latter live in districts nearer to Central London. There was a contrast, among the sons and daughters I called on, between the homes. Some lived in three rooms in a Victorian terraced street in East Ham, or in a new council flat in the East End, overlooking a dusty children's playground. Others had bought their houses—a bungalow high up near Leigh-on-Sea, with a view over the Thames and the routes used by the cargo ships bound for Ford's or for the East London docks; a Tudor-style house in Gidea Park; a semi-detached house in a newer private estate on the outskirts of Chelmsford, with unmade roads and the nearest school a 20-minute walk away.

The self-selecting process

It seems, from the interviews in homes like these and from the other evidence, that there has from the beginning been a constant process of self-selection among the population of the Dagenham estate. This process has tended to remove people, among tenants and the children of tenants, of two main kinds—those in professional and white-collar jobs and those who, though manual workers, have both the means and the aspiration to 'better themselves'. Terence Young remarked on this in 1934; as well as the poorer people who moved back to London, he said, there were also the 'higher ranges' who 'moved to purchased houses'.[1] This has been noted in other housing estate studies as well.[2]

Talking to the voluntary emigrants among the sons and daughters in their new homes, I was struck by the sense of a continuous outward movement from inner London—a process which had taken people from Wapping to Dagenham as children, and then on to Basildon or South Benfleet in adult life. Some of the emigrants themselves commented on this. One son said about the estate at Hockley where he now lives:

'We moved to Dagenham from Stepney when I was six. It seemed so much better—fresh air, more open, much better houses. Now this place seems to me better than Dagenham, just like Dagenham used to seem better than Stepney.'

This chapter, to sum up, shows that in yet another respect the estate is very much like the older communities. From Dagenham, as from the East End itself, certain kinds of people—the socially mobile, the ambitious, the aspiring— often move away. This voluntary outward migration is something, incidentally, which those who write about the 'population stability' of the traditional communities some- times neglect—I think we rather did this in *Family and Kinship in East London*. The population of Bethnal Green itself, for instance, fell by more than half between 1931 and

[1] Young, T., op. cit., p. 217. See also p. 240.
[2] See Durant, R., *Watling*, p. 18, and Williams, N., op. cit., p. 22. And Jevons and Madge said, of those who left the Bristol housing estates they studied: 'The tenants who had left and who could be subsequently traced to interview proved to belong very largely to the better-off class on the estates . . . foremen, manual workers in supervisory positions and black-coated workers together composed 54% of all leavers interviewed. Black-coated workers, never very numerous on the estates, showed the greatest tendency to leave.' Jevons, R., and Madge, J., *Housing Estates*, p. 44. The reasons for leaving were also familiar, '. . . the principal reason given for leaving was dislike of the estate as such, and particu- larly the dislike of neighbours. The population was said to be too mixed.' Ibid., p. 68.

1961. Part of this drop can be explained by the war, part by Dagenham and the other housing estates built before and after 1945. But many of those who went must have left for similar reasons as the voluntary expatriates from the Dagenham estate. These people left both districts because their native locality could not offer what they wanted, in type or quality of housing and in other ways. Amongst other things, the relative uniformity of the population of Dagenham and Bethnal Green alike—its overwhelmingly working-class character—drove away the socially mobile among them. As an ex-Dagenham son, a surveyor now living at Gidea Park, put it, 'The people there were not conversationalists. They were just working-class people who lived from day to day. I was determined to get out as soon as I could.'

What has happened at Dagenham is that just because the place is a vast one-class colony, many of the people who have 'moved up in the world' have also moved away. Their continuous emigration has both been caused by social uniformity and has helped to perpetuate it. This process, at least as important as the kind of involuntary movement discussed in the previous chapter, has done much to define the estate's character.

VI

FRIENDS AND NEIGHBOURS

IN its class make-up and to some extent in its kinship patterns, Dagenham is much like the older communities from which it was recruited. I now want to look at the patterns of relationships that have developed with the other residents on the estate.

First, in general terms most people apparently think their fellows 'friendly'. The people in the marriage sample were asked explicitly for their opinion on the friendliness or otherwise, first of the street they lived in, then of the estate as a whole, and to both questions less than a fifth made criticisms of unfriendliness (of the 100 husbands and wives, only 18 thought their street, 13 the estate generally, 'unfriendly'). In the new estate of Greenleigh, by contrast, well over half the people interviewed had complained that the others were unfriendly. This is a trivial index in itself, of course, but it does suggest an atmosphere of greater amicability at Dagenham.

There is a similar contrast in people's contacts with each other, at least when these are measured in terms of visitors into the home. It is not possible to make a direct statistical comparison, because the questions were asked in different ways in the two estates—at Dagenham, people in the marriage sample were asked about the number of visits to or from friends or neighbours in the previous *week*; at Greenleigh, in the previous *month*.[1] But, since two in five of the people at Greenleigh had been visitors or been visited, in

---

[1] People in the general sample at Dagenham were asked about visits, by friends or neighbours, into their own home during the previous 24 hours; 30% had received at least one.

the previous month, compared with three in five at Dagenham in the shorter period, there is no doubt about the difference.

It is easy to see why the old estate might be different from the new. 'We all moved in together and our children have grown up here. We know most of the people and so naturally we get on all right with them,' as Mrs. Millwood put it. Mrs. Wright said, 'This estate is established and so it's more of a friendly place.'

The patterns of visiting

To say that Dagenham is 'more friendly' than a new estate like Greenleigh, and that more people have friends or neighbours into their homes, tells one very little about the sort of social relationships that have developed. Who are these visitors, and what happens when they call?

First, most visits, it turns out, are not formal, pre-arranged affairs. There is at Dagenham very little regular 'entertaining' of friends—to a meal, for an evening's talk or television, or to a party—such as goes on amongst professional and managerial people. Most meetings inside people's homes take the form of 'popping in' for a chat or to give or to receive day-to-day aid. 'My friend across the road always pops in here if she's going shopping,' said Mrs. Lee, 'but we don't sit about with each other in the afternoon, and she doesn't come in here at night when my husband's home.'

For most people the circle of friends who visit is quite small. Of the husbands and wives in the marriage sample who had exchanged visits in the previous seven days, over half had done so with only one person and another quarter with only two. Women who reported that they had both made and received five visits often went on to explain that all were with one person—'my friend over the road'.

These contacts are between women much more than men. Of the 50 wives in the marriage sample, 42 had visited or been visited at least once in the previous week, compared with 20 of their husbands. This is, of course, because the women are, on the whole, home much more often in the daytime.[1] But even though the wives who go out to work have rather less visitors than those who do not, the differences are not very great.[2] The truth seems to be that going out to work can, for the women, influence their relationships with others in two contrary ways. Some wives who work certainly have less visitors. One of them is Mrs. Johnstone. 'I'm out all day,' she said, 'so I don't really get to know the neighbours.' Mrs. Ralph works from 8.30 a.m. to 4 p.m., soldering coils at a large radio and television factory at Ilford. 'I don't have a lot to do with the other women,' she explained, 'I'm out at work every day and I haven't time to stand and jaw. I don't very often see them, except Saturdays up at the shops.'

Other working wives regularly exchange visits with friends nearby who help with their children. Just as women without paid employment lamented that, though they had tried, they had not been able to find jobs at hours which would enable them to fulfil their responsibilities to their children, others explained that they had been able to take jobs, although having school-age children, just because ready assistance was at hand. Mrs. Roberts was one. 'Mrs. Bacon next door pays my rent, does the bagwash and puts it out to dry,' she said, 'I know if the children come home she'll be there to see to them.' Mrs. Palmer explained:

'The children are on their own for about half an hour, from half past four till five, when I get home from work, but they're always in full view of the neighbours. If they want anything

[1] Of the married, widowed and divorced women in the general sample, 17% were working full time, and another 17% part time. Comparisons with Bethnal Green and Woodford are as follows. Women working full time in Bethnal Green 27%, Woodford 11%; part time, in Bethnal Green 16%, Woodford 14%. In this matter Dagenham is thus somewhere between Woodford, where most housewives do not seek outside employment, and Bethnal Green, where local conditions—small clothing workshops and the like, and office-cleaning jobs in the nearby City—provide relatively better employment opportunities than at Dagenham.

[2] Proportions visited by a non-relative in the previous 24 hours: married and widowed women working full-time, 24%; part-time, 30%; not working outside the home, 34% (General sample).

Mrs. Jordan over the road sees to it for them. Mrs. Jordan gets the groceries for us.'

In other words, if going out to work keeps some wives apart, for others it is made possible by their being together already. And the practical help the wives receive in this situation provides one illustration of the kind of neighbourly give and take that goes on.

The local network

The people who help, in this and other ways, live close at hand. There are exceptions. Mrs. Davies said, 'I've got one friend who comes in. She's not a neighbour. We speak to the neighbours, but that's all. My friend lives on the estate, about ten minutes' walk away. She comes for tea once a week and I go round to her. It's a regular thing. I met her through the children going to the same religious classes.' Mrs. Barton said likewise, 'I've got a friend round in York Avenue. Every week I go round to her one afternoon and she comes here another. I used to work with her back in Stepney before I was married and we kept in touch after we moved here.'

For most people, however, it is not like this. In fact, the radius of friendship is extremely localized. Apart from relatives, people seldom seem to maintain contact with, or exchange visits with, others if they do not live close at hand. Most of the friends who visit them are drawn from amongst people living in the dozen or so houses nearby. The friendships that bring wives, and to a lesser extent husbands, into each other's homes are of a piece with the day-to-day meetings in the garden or street. 'I see Mrs. Jones every day to speak to,' said Mrs. Knight; 'she doesn't come in as a rule, but we walk up to the shops together, or like today when the laundry called and I went over to pay her and stopped for a little chat.' And Mrs. Taylor explained, 'Mrs. Braddock lives next door. We go shopping together near enough every day and we go to the school together to collect the children. She doesn't come in much; she usually calls me over the back there and we have a talk over the garden fence.'

Of course, people choose their friends, but they usually choose them from among people they see often as neighbours. Frequently, the friends who are selected live next door or across the road.[1]

'I know the women on either side best,' said Mrs. Salmon, 'because they're the ones I mostly see. Sometimes they come in here or I go in there.'

Mrs. Gibson's closest friends are two of her neighbours.

'We've got some good friends, particularly Mrs. Gordon over the road and Mrs. Wheeler who lives just down the street. If I'm ever fed up I go in to Mrs. Gordon for a friendly cup of tea and a chat and then we go to Mrs. Wheeler, the three of us are just like that.'

The links between the women are not only those of companionship, but are often built upon mutual aid in their day-to-day tasks. Mrs. Page has a friend living two doors away.

'If we happen to run short,' she said, 'we always run in to each other, and if she ever buys anything excessive she asks me to use it up. If I go out she sees to the workmen or the laundry man or the rent man, and I do the same for her. If you needed her help she'd always be there.'

'I've got two very good friends,' Mrs. Jarvis said. 'Mrs. Barker, who lives opposite, has got a spin drier and I've got a sewing machine. I put my washing in her spin drier and she uses my sewing machine when she wants to. Then the lady next door on one side is another friend of mine. We always help each other out.'

---

[1] Other studies have made this point—that people's friends are often drawn from their immediate neighbours. For example: '. . . each informant's active neighbourly relations were confined within a very small radius, representing that section of the street in which she lived.' Hole, V., op. cit., p. 167. A study carried out in 1951–2 of a Sheffield estate, remarked, 'Housewives' relationships were usually made with their next-door neighbours, those living within 20 or 30 yards, and residents in the same street.' Mitchell, G. D., *et al.*, op. cit., p. 109. See also Willmott, P., 'Housing Density and Town Design in a New Town' (Stevenage), p. 125.

The men have less to do with each other, but often their friendships, too, develop out of shared interests around the home. Apart from an occasional trade union meeting, most men seem to see little of their workmates outside working hours. Even when people share their employer, or even their job, as well as their residence on the estate, they do not apparently have much to do with each other unless they also live very near. Contacts like this are common:

'We hadn't been here a fortnight,' said Mr. Gray, 'when the turf that I'd ordered came, and I had the job of putting it down. The chappie down at the bottom of the garden came and said, "Why don't you borrow my fork?" Then when I started to do it, he said, "Let me help you." It turned out that that was his line of business. He's quite a pal of mine now. He helps me with the garden; I help him with photography; it's my hobby and he's just taking it up.'

Mr. Dover's great hobby is woodwork; at the time he was interviewed he was busy on a pelmet he was making for a friend living next door and he had just finished a toy train for the son of another. He relies on Fred, another friend who is also a neighbour, to help when needed. 'Just today I was sawing a log for the engine of this train and Fred sees that my saw is blunt and lends me a sharp one. Anything at all I want he'll lend it to me if he has it. I'm the same with him. The other day he knocked when I wasn't here and borrowed my steps—we take each other for granted that way.'

How do these patterns tie in with those with relatives, described earlier? Some people live in the thick of extended families, others are isolated from kin. Some people, it is now apparent, have friends among their neighbours with whom they give and receive help. What is the connexion? Have friends taken the place of relatives for the couples whose kindred are not near?

It is not like this. Some couples, of course, have friends at hand, but not relatives. Others have relatives nearby and see little of other people, and others see little of either. But many both belong to extended families and have a good deal to do with their neighbours as well. Mrs. Rank often has neighbours in; her mother also lives round the corner and is seen every day. She is not unique. Of the 209 people in the general sample who had been visited by relatives in the previous 24 hours, 37% had also been visited by friends or neighbours, against 28% of the 668 who had not been visited by relatives. The two kinds of relationship, in other words, are not mutually exclusive. On the contrary, those with relatives at hand are rather more likely to have friends in their homes as well. This is exactly what we found in Bethnal Green also.[1]

'Friends' and 'friendliness'

Two main points have been established so far in this chapter. Most people at Dagenham regard the other residents as 'friendly'. And most people have got 'friends' on the estate, in the sense that other people, living nearby, come into their homes. In these two ways Dagenham is certainly a more sociable place than the newer estate of Greenleigh. But how does it compare with the older working-class communities like Bethnal Green?

Let me look at the two aspects in turn. The fact that people at Dagenham say, in answer to a general question, that the others are 'friendly' does not in itself show very much. People say the same in Bethnal Green, it is true. But they also do so in middle-class Woodford, whose patterns are in other ways not at all like those of the East End. In fact, a majority of informants would probably give the same answer in almost any district except brand-new housing estates and the like. Nor is the presence of friends in the home a characteristic which Dagenham shares with the other working-class areas. Unfortunately, no direct statistical comparison can be made between the estate and Bethnal Green on this, because the question was not put in our earlier research. But the impression from the Bethnal

[1] See *Family and Kinship in East London*, p. 84.

Green surveys and those in similar kinds of district is that this kind of visiting is not common,[1] and that the social life of the older communities depends, apart from frequent visiting between relatives, much more upon a multiplicity of contacts *outside* the home with others living in the district.

It seems to me, therefore, important to distinguish between two concepts. The first is 'friendship', in the sense of having friends (who are often neighbours as well) into the home. The second is 'friendliness', in the sense of the kind of informal, generalized 'matiness' which characterizes the old East End communities. In Bethnal Green and such districts people may have few 'friends' in the former sense, yet they find the place extremely 'friendly'. The reason is that so many fellow residents are familiar; they are, at a different level, 'friends' of long standing; they are the people who have for years been seen and chatted to daily in the street, the pub, the corner shop or at the market.

How far has this kind of matiness grown up at Dagenham? Trying to answer this question presented about the most contradictory evidence I had met in research at Dagenham or anywhere else. People's opinions differed so sharply. So great were the divergences that it was sometimes as if informants who lived a few hundred yards from each other were talking about entirely different districts. Their attitudes depended a good deal, of course, upon their actual dealings with others in the locality—upon how many they knew, how well they knew them and how much they had to do with them. And it is possible to distinguish a small minority and two larger groups.

The minority were extremely isolated—they had no friends nearby, did not know the names of or talk to their neighbours in the garden or in the street, and so on. These were the kind of people who firmly said their fellows were 'unfriendly', and who amounted to less than a fifth of the people in the marriage sample.

[1] See Bakke, E. W., *The Unemployed Man*, pp. 153-4; Mogey, J. M., op. cit., pp. 83-87; Kerr, M., op. cit., pp. 101-8.

The majority were divided fairly evenly, as far as I could judge from what they said in the interviews, into two views. One described social relationships at Dagenham as 'friendly' but somewhat distant.

> 'In Bow it's Auntie this and Auntie that. Here it's Mr. and Mrs. to the neighbours. They're friendly but not familiar.'

> 'It's friendly here, but more reserved. There's no animosity or anything like that. But people keep themselves to themselves more. When they're home, they're home—their doors are closed.'

Such people distinguished sharply between their 'friends'— that is those out of the people living nearby with whom they might exchange visits or go shopping—and the rest of the neighbours. Mrs. Snell said, 'I don't mix with many of the neighbours. The women on both sides and the woman opposite—they're my friends. I say "Good morning" to the others, but that's all.' Mrs. Pink was another; 'My only friend round here is Mrs. Noble. The rest are just neighbours—we hardly speak.'

Not, they insisted, that neighbours at Dagenham are unhelpful to each other. 'Underneath that aloofness,' said one man, 'they're every bit as helpful when you need it.' But there are limits to sociability, boundaries to neighbourliness.

> 'It's English friendliness. One nods one's head. Of course, we know the people round here, but there's no real friendliness until you're ill or something like that.'

> 'The neighbours we had in Stepney were always ready for a laugh or a joke, more easy-going than here.'

> 'It's a different atmosphere here altogether—much better for the children. But they're not the matey type you get in Poplar.'

The pattern of relationships these people describe—more 'reserved', more 'aloof', 'not so familiar'—is close to the stereotype of 'suburban' social life. And indeed, apart from the fact that people in the middle-class suburb of Woodford had friends in their homes more often,[1] and tended to draw at least some of them from farther afield, the relationships of many of these Dagenham residents seem similar. 'Dagenham is like the other suburban areas in this way,' said one man, who put it, I should explain, more strongly than most. 'They suffer from the same common factor—suburbanitis, a withdrawing, a shutting of the door.'

What was described by the other main group of informants at Dagenham was not at all like suburbia; it was like Bethnal Green. They saw the estate differently—or at least the part where they lived—and apparently had very different relationships with those living near them. They might have special 'friends', but they did not distinguish so sharply between them and the others. 'We're all good pals round here,' said Mrs. Croom. 'Everybody's very friendly with everybody else in this little community.' Some explicitly drew the parallel between their present social relations and those of the East End.

'We're the East End type round here,' said Mrs. Dover. 'Everybody's friendly. We all know each other, we all help each other. The wives who go out to work, all the others help them with their kiddies, or paying their rent, or seeing the baker for them. And then we often have parties along here that we all go to.'

Mr. Adams, who had arrived from Shoreditch in 1927, thought that time had re-created the spirit of the old district:

'At the beginning the atmosphere was more of the off-handed, but now it's more of the amicable. At first people weren't bold enough—they didn't like to speak to each other—but after a while they began to speak and get more friendly. Now Dagenham has moulded itself into a place where most people know each other. The atmosphere has originated itself to more or less what it was back in Shoreditch.'

[1] See Table 19, in Appendix 2, which compares the classes in both districts.

This chapter, to conclude, has shown that relationships between residents at Dagenham have developed beyond the stage reached in post-1945 Greenleigh. But the more important question I asked about Dagenham—has it re-created the social atmosphere of the East End—cannot be answered. Because for every Mrs. Dover who thinks it has there is a Mrs. Pink who thinks it has not. The reasons for this disagreement are discussed in the next chapter.

VII

VARIATIONS IN SOCIABILITY

THE question raised by the previous chapter is why some people see the estate so differently, and have such different dealings with their neighbours. The issue is not so much about variations in 'friendships' inside the home as about how people living nearby get on outside it. In this chapter I examine what seem to me some of the explanations.

One influence is time—how long people have lived on the estate. 'I don't know anybody,' said Mrs. Hunter, who had been at Dagenham for three years, 'I hardly speak to a soul except for the children from the time my husband goes off to work in the morning until he comes home at night. Here, unless you're one of those who've been here 40 years, you're an outsider.' Other new-comers shared these views. Of the 48 men and women in the marriage sample who had moved to the estate since 1945, a third said that their street was 'unfriendly', compared with only two of the 52 who had arrived earlier. It should be added that a few of the older tenants found the social atmosphere of their street 'unfriendly', just because it contained so many new immigrants. One of them, Mrs. Powell, said, 'As new people have moved in, the spirit has changed. All the old people used to know each other, and I still know a lot, but it's not as friendly with all these new people from Bow.'

But if more of the new-comers complain about the attitudes of their fellows, this is not reflected in their behaviour inside their homes. Of the 24 wives in the marriage sample, for instance, who had arrived since 1945, eight had been visited by non-relatives four or more times in the previous week, as had eight of the 26 who went to Dagenham earlier; and ten of the first group of wives, like nine of the second, had been visited by only one or by none. In other words, there was virtually no difference between the two groups.[1]

The contrast, again, is between 'having friends in' and 'friendliness'; the people who had lived on the estate longer might have no more visitors, but they tended, for obvious reasons, to know more of the people they met outside the home. 'When I come along from the shops,' said Mrs. Mitchell, 'everybody sort of stops and has a chat because they've known me since I was a little girl.' 'We know all the people in this turning,' said Mr. Gale, 'They're mostly old neighbours.' Mrs. Rank explained, 'You've got a lot of the same neighbours as you've had all along. People's children have grown up and got married. The parents have lived down here for a long time and you've seen them right through it all.'

Others also had noticed, what has been observed in other districts, that the children had often eased the course of friendship for the older residents. 'I started talking to the neighbours when my children went to school,' said Mrs. Kemp, now 64, who came in 1927, 'You start talking to the other mothers when you're waiting outside the school. And then later on, as your children are growing up, people stop you and tell you "My daughter is getting married" and that sort of thing. You've more or less all gone through it together.' Mrs. Salmon, a younger wife who had herself come to Dagenham as a little girl, said, 'They all had their children about the same age. Their children were young when I was young. We all grew up together.'

Of course, many of the new-comers, too, had got to know other people through children or in other ways. And I do not want to give the impression that all the recent immigrants complained about their fellows. After all, though a

[1] This applies to the general sample also. See Tables 20 and 21, in Appendix 2, which show that neither people who have been on the estate, nor in their present homes, for relatively short periods receive less visits than those who have been there longer.

third said the other people in their street were 'unfriendly', two-thirds did not. Mr. Roberts, who had arrived four years earlier, said he had found the established residents hospitable —'They're ever so friendly here, they're good neighbours. When we first arrived, we thought we'd have to enquire what shops to use and all that, but the neighbours took the wife round. The woman next door cooked our meals on her gas stove for the first week—when we hadn't got one. They couldn't have been more helpful.' Mrs. Pippin, who had come in 1952, said, 'We find the people here very friendly. Our neighbours have always been helpful. We were made very welcome when we first came.' But these people's experiences do not undermine the main conclusion—that the length of time residents have lived at Dagenham can, for some, be part of the explanation for the coolness they report.

Conflicts between generations

Another influence, connected with this, is people's age in relation to that of their neighbours. Older people whose neighbours were young couples with children sometimes found them uncongenial and had little to do with them. 'There are so many young people round here now,' said Mrs. Lee, 'They think they can come down here and run the place. They're always rowing and their children are so cheeky and rude.' 'People with children,' said Mrs. Bird, 'don't seem to want to bother with older people. We don't know many of them.'

The younger people complained in their turn. Mrs. Palmer said, 'They're set in their ways.' Mrs. Gibson agreed —'They're all too old on this estate. They get into a state about the children playing and shouting. If there were more young people here this estate would be friendlier.'

This suggests that, particularly where the house designs and street layout do not protect people adequately against intrusion of one form or another—against, for instance, the noise of children playing, or against children running into

71

gardens—there may well be tensions between the generations. This was noted also by the authors of the Sheffield
housing estate study, who remarked on 'the friction which
undoubtedly exists at times between the elderly and the rest
of the community'.[1]

It is clear, however, from the Dagenham interviews that
strains like these are less likely where the old people have
known the younger for some years—for instance, where the
married daughter of an old neighbour has taken over her
parents' tenancy—and, even less, when they are related.
Old people, it is obvious, have a greater tolerance for—and
more influence over—their own grandchildren than other
people's; and it seems likely that, if their grandchildren are
amongst those living nearby, they will feel more tolerant
towards young children generally. Kinship, in other words,
makes it easy for the generations to live together; its absence
often makes it difficult.

Difference in status

Another thing that seems to affect people's attitudes to,
and familiarity with, their neighbours is whether they think
of them as being of a similar social status to themselves.
Dagenham is relatively homogeneous in terms of people's
jobs, as has been shown earlier. What is more, there do not
seem to be major variations in social behaviour as between,
for instance, skilled and unskilled workers.[2] But, just the
same, there *are* differences, and a few people are keenly
aware of them.

Some of these differences are to do with occupation. One
man explained, 'I'm a printer. Most of the people round here
just work at Ford's. I haven't got much in common with
these people; there's no conversation at all. You see, they
don't come from my walk of life. I've got just a few friends
on the estate and that's the finish.' Other things have an
influence as well as occupation; income or the number of

[1] Mitchell, G. D., *et al.*, op. cit., p. 111. See also p. 120.
[2] See Table 22, on 'Social Class and Social Contacts', in Appendix 2.

young children in the family, for example, or more elusive differences in attitudes and aspirations of the kind which researchers have distinguished as marking off from each other the 'aspiring' people, the 'respectable' and the 'rough'.[1]

Whatever the basis of differentiation, some people—about one in ten of those in the marriage sample—think themselves socially superior to those living near them, and apparently keep aloof. These are, not surprisingly, often the very people, mentioned in Chapter V, who wish to get away from the estate. Here I am not concerned with their reasons for wanting to go but their attitudes to their present neighbours. 'Friendly?' said one of them. 'Too much so, if you ask me. There are people round here I wouldn't care to mix with.' He went on:

> 'We like to live a bit decent and I'm afraid that's what we don't agree with about this place. Not everybody has got the same idea. And I'm afraid some of the people here think we're a bit too high and mighty for them.'

Another man said:

> 'You've got to admit this estate is low class. I don't go on the other people here myself. As far as intellect goes, they haven't got much intellect. Things are getting worse here. The social standard of the other residents had just begun to rise, but now they've been dragged back to where they started from. There are families here now—I don't know how they get the houses —who bring their environment with them. You can't stop the children mixing and so it spreads.'

A clerk's wife also distinguished herself and her family from her fellow residents.

> 'We try to stop Linda playing with the children next door. Most of the children round here speak real cockney, they're really common. The parents don't seem to want to better themselves or their children. We try not to have much to do with them.'

---

[1] Unfortunately, there has not been agreement on terms or definitions. See, e.g. Kuper, L., op. cit., pp. 80–82; Mogey, J. M., op cit., pp. 140–5; Mitchell, G. D. *et al.,* op. cit., p. 106; Stacey, M., *Tradition and Change,* p. 153; and Jennings, H., op. cit., p. 221.

There were others, very few, who had little contact with neighbours for the opposite reason—they felt they were ostracized by them. One woman said, 'They are not at all friendly round here. They all seem to think they're better than us. We've offered to help and they've refused. Sometimes they speak and sometimes they don't. They blow hot and cold. They just don't want to be friendly; they're independent. We don't even say "Good morning" to half of them.' And another remarked, 'They're too snooty to want to talk to us.'

It is not simply that some Dagenham residents exclude themselves, or are excluded, from a general 'friendliness' because they do not 'fit in' with those living nearby. Quite apart from this, there are variations in the importance people give to 'reserve' in itself. And from the remarks of informants, it seems that white-collar workers and some of the 'aspiring' manual workers value it more highly than others. 'It's the more modern way,' said a foreman who was explaining that he did not believe in being 'too friendly' with others.

Differences in streets

I have been discussing so far differences between individuals which might help to explain variations in 'friendliness' with neighbours. I have suggested some of the influences that keep people apart from their fellows, and indicated that, while some maintain their distance because they want to, others seem to be less content with their relative isolation. These last include some of the newcomers living among established residents, or of the old people living among young.

If I am right in my interpretation, the extent to which people are 'reserved' or not can also be influenced by the kind of street they live in. There are manifest differences in the appearance of different streets, and in what I can only describe as their 'atmosphere'. Compare, for example, a broad main road busy with cars and buses and heavy lorries, or even a less noisy but still wide, straight avenue, with a secluded cul-de-sac of 12 houses or a short, narrow side street of 40, free from traffic except delivery vans and the cars of some of the tenants. One is a broad thoroughfare in which the sheer width and the traffic flow effectively separate the houses on opposite sides, so that they do not, in any sense, belong together. The other is more intimate, the macadam only a parenthesis between sets of facing houses that clearly share common membership of some sort of physical unity.

People were aware of this difference themselves, and some of those who lived in the more closely built streets thought they had a distinctive *social* atmosphere as well. This seemed particularly true of people living in the 'banjos' (cul-de-sacs).[1] Though the numbers in such roads were small—only nine couples, of the 50 in the marriage sample, lived in them[2]—the strong impression from the interviews was that the people in 'banjos' were on friendly, easy-going terms with their fellows, in a way reminiscent of the little streets of Bethnal Green.

'We know everybody in this part,' said Mrs. Carson, who lives in a cul-de-sac. 'Everybody's friendly. They will always do a good turn. If you're queer or anything like that, they'll knock at your door and say, "Don't go out today; I'll do your shopping for you." '

'In this banjo,' said Mrs. Croom, 'when one of the neighbour's children married a little while ago we all rallied round. They all came back here—we cleared the room and put up tables for the reception—and then we went to another house on the banjo for a "knees-up". That's what we're like here. Everybody's neighbourly, everybody helps. Oh, there's so much help in this little banjo of ours that I can't describe it all.'

'They are all very nice in this turning,' said Mrs. Farley, who also lives in a 'banjo'. 'If anybody wants anything done we'll

[1] See the disgram on p. xiv, for examples of 'banjos' and other street types.
[2] The proportion of people in the general sample as a whole living in 'banjos' was even smaller—9%.

all sort of muck in and help. If people want the gas man let in, or if anybody's ill and wants some shopping done, or anything like that, we all sort of help one another.'

There seemed a similar atmosphere, too, in some other streets, mostly those which were relatively narrow and were either short in themselves, or were effectively made short by intersecting roads. Mr. Williams, who lived in one of the latter, spoke warmly of the friendliness of 'this turning', and when asked how he defined 'turning', explained, 'from the top of the road down to where Dacres Road crosses it' (a distance of about 150 yards). He had decided that he did not want to move away.

> 'We have thought of moving,' he said, 'because, of course, they are 1919 houses really—they haven't got the amenities you get in a modern house. But weighing it all up, because of knowing all our neighbours so well here, we've decided not to move. They're so friendly and helpful in this turning, all good friends.'

Mr. Harrison, who lived in a short, narrow road, was also reluctant to move.

> 'They're very friendly in this street,' he said, 'we know nearly all of them. If they thought you were in trouble they'd go out of their way to help. There's nothing they wouldn't do. I'd hate to leave this little street.'

The fact that remarks like this came so often from people in these sorts of street does not mean that a similar atmosphere never develops elsewhere on the estate; Mr. and Mrs. Hodgson live in a terrace of 12 houses in a main road which, although physically very different, seems in spirit much like the 'banjos'—'We know everybody along here,' said Mrs. Hodgson; 'I mean in the houses on each side of us in this little block. Everyone's invited to parties and do's and that. And if anyone's queer or anything, they all help.' But despite examples of this kind, there did seem a clear pattern in people's responses to the question—asked of those in the marriage sample—about the friendliness of their street. None of the people living in 'banjos' thought the others in their street 'unfriendly'; a fifth of those in other roads did.

What is it about a street that helps to make for this difference in atmosphere? First, there is the extent to which it is physically marked off from others. It is easier for people to think of it as 'our street', to develop a sense of identity with it and with the other people there, if it is physically 'framed' than if it has no obvious beginning or end. The 'banjos' at Dagenham certainly have a clear physical identity, and to some extent the same applies to many of the other 'friendly' streets. 'When you talk about friends,' a man in a side road said, 'I'm only talking about this little row of houses here, down to the corner, and the row opposite.' Mrs. Salmon, living in a longer avenue, drew a contrast with Poplar, where she had previously lived:

> 'Apart from people on either side of you, you're only on good-morning terms with the rest. But when we lived in Poplar it was a small turning. There were only about 40 houses in the turning and everybody knew each other.'

This difference has been observed in other research. The study of the Sheffield estate, already referred to, concluded that:

> 'The street as a whole is . . . a most important reference point for social activity. . . . If it has not more than about a hundred houses the residents will probably know something about everybody who lives in it. In a longer road the number of people who are identified in this way will depend upon the housing layout and the movements of the residents within it. On a main thoroughfare much less interest is taken in the road as a whole.'[1]

[1] Mitchell, G. D., *et al.*, op. cit., p. 106. It may also be significant that on the Liverpool housing estate described in the same book the 'friendliest' of the three 'blocks' investigated was called 'Shakespeare Close'. One wonders if it was, in fact, the only one of the three which was a cul-de-sac. Certainly the remarks of one woman quoted were reminiscent of those of people in Dagenham banjos— 'I get on well with them. I am friendly with my next-door neighbours and I know everyone in the Close.' Ibid., p. 56.

The second feature of the 'friendly' streets is the physical arrangement of the houses themselves. Their relationship to each other, and the access-routes in and out of the street, are such as to make frequent chance meetings between neighbours more likely than in other forms of layout. The compact, inward-facing form of the 'banjos', and, to a lesser extent, the relative narrowness of some of the side streets, are conducive to meetings of this kind. And it is out of these that more lasting relationships between neighbours often develop.

There is a more general point here—that of housing density. The closer houses are to each other, the more frequently the local neighbours are likely to see and meet each other. Dagenham has 12 houses to the acre, compared with something like 40 in an old-style East End street, and Mrs. Bradshaw for one thought this was a reason for the difference in social relationships:

> 'We know the immediate neighbours, that's all. We don't know the people along the street. I think it's because people are more apart here. The houses are spaced out more and so you don't get to know each other so well. Where we lived up in Shoreditch we lived in just one little turning, and our street door was next to the next person's street door. In the summer all the doors were open—you couldn't help meeting each other and talking to each other.'

Mrs. Hayward agreed:

> 'You don't have all that much to do with other people here, because you don't see them so much. There's more separation between the houses here—they're not so close to each other as they are in London. Because of that people don't mingle so much. You're not so close to each other.'

Privacy and conflicts

Not, of course, that it follows automatically that people who are brought together by the physical design will necessarily get on with each other. There was some evidence at Dagenham that the opposite could happen—the most obvious example being over shared front porches. No doubt for reasons of economy or aesthetics, rather than out of any intention to promote sociability, the L.C.C. built something like a quarter of the houses—both in the cul-de-sacs and in the estate generally—with a shared porch which acts as shelter to the two adjacent front doors; there is no division between the two, and the tiled or cemented step is also shared. Here next-door neighbours are forced into so close a relationship, and so much dependence upon each other over cleaning, for instance, that there is potential strain. If they get on well, then the shared porch is a means to even greater co-operation. But if they do not, the strains may lead to open conflict.

> 'I don't like sharing the porch,' said one wife. 'This morning I was scrubbing my side of the porch and I thought I'd better scrub hers as well to make it look all the same, and she came out and said, "Why do you have to scrub my half?" Well, she's found out I *won't* quarrel, I never will quarrel, and I didn't say anything. I suppose it made her angry, because she banged me on the top of the head with a broom. Well, I thought, I'm not going to put up with that, so I paid her. I hit her back. I don't like that sort of thing—we want to have our own front door.'

Mrs. Adams had changed her house because of trouble over the porch:

> 'I was under a porch and I had such a bad neighbour. She was very unfriendly. She swore, too, terrible language. My little girl used to hide by the gate when she came home from school. She wouldn't come in while the woman was there. So I decided to move.'

And Mrs. Kemp was anxious because her next-door neighbour was going to move away. 'It sets me worrying,' she said, 'who I'm going to get in the same porch. I've always got on well with her, but you don't know about another person, do you?'[1]

---

[1] The porches at Dagenham have apparently generated tensions all along. Young remarked that they were 'sometimes a source of considerable friction between

Of course, most people who were sharing porches got on well with their neighbours. But it is nonetheless true that a physical design which promotes contacts may generate conflicts as well as goodwill, and some local officials suggested that the cul-de-sacs themselves were regarded with disfavour by many tenants just because they led to too much contact with neighbours. They told me that people wanting to transfer out of cul-de-sacs often say apologetically that their present street is 'only a banjo', just as others applying for transfers often write uncompromisingly 'no banjos'.

This might suggest that there is a good deal of discontent among the people living in cul-de-sacs, but there is no evidence that this is so. The (small) proportion of people in the marriage sample, for instance, who wanted to leave the estate was much the same in main roads, side roads and cul-de-sacs alike. Nor did we come across anybody, in the marriage or tenants' samples, who complained about the 'banjos' being too sociable, or who had moved away into a different sort of street on these grounds. Nor is there any evidence of greater mobility in the cul-de-sacs.[1]

It is clear, however, that some transfers, from one sort of street to another on the estate, do take place, and it looks, for instance, as if the 'banjos' contain rather less white-collar people, and rather less older people[2]—both groups who might prefer more seclusion than a 'banjo' would provide—than do other kinds of street. But, though a certain amount of this self-selection undoubtedly goes on, and does something to account for the differences in 'matiness' between one street and another, this is, I am

---

neighbours'. Young, T., op. cit., p. 106. And when Mass-Observation carried out its interviews there in the early 1940s, 28% of the people with shared porches spontaneously complained about them. The stories were familiar. 'It's terrible, the rows with these porches. Last week I saw the woman over the way having a set-to with her neighbour on the step.' Mass-Observation, op. cit., pp. 123, 172.

[1] See Table 23, in Appendix 2.
[2] See Tables 24 and 25, in Appendix 2.

sure, not the sole explanation for the variations. The physical layout of streets, in itself, has a big influence on the relationships between the people who live there.

The suggestion that the physical arrangement of housing can influence social relationships is not new. A series of studies, mostly American, have come to the same conclusion—and about the relative 'friendliness' of cul-de-sacs (or 'courts' as the Americans call them) in particular. One of the authors of an American study, of two housing 'projects' for ex-servicemen, put its conclusions like this:

> 'It is a fair summary to say that two major factors affecting the friendships that developed were (1) sheer distance between the houses and (2) the direction in which a house faced. . . . Because of the arrangement of the courts in the housing project, these two factors combined to make it easy for social groups to develop within the court. . . .'[1]

What has also been shown by that study, and by many others, is that the physical arrangement is more likely to work in this kind of way if the residents are similar kinds of people than if they are not. If neighbours feel very different from each other and do not want to mix, such layouts may indeed exacerbate social conflicts.[2] As Kuper put it in his study of a Coventry housing estate, 'Whether more friendly relations will result from a particular layout depends not only on the opportunities for contact, but on the people themselves, their attitudes to each other, and their compatibility with each other'.[3]

This can be confirmed from Dagenham: the first part of this chapter was, in fact, concerned with the differences

---

[1] Festinger, L., 'Architecture and Group Membership', p. 156. The fuller report of the study will be found in Festinger, L., Schachter, S., and Back, K., *Social Pressures in Informal Groups*. See also Merton, R. K. 'The social psychology of housing', pp. 203–9; Whyte, W. H., *The Organization Man,* pp. 336–49; Caplow, T., and Foreman, R., 'Neighbourhood Interaction in a Homogeneous Community', pp. 357–66; Kuper, L., op. cit., pp. 1–202. These studies are critically examined by Gans, H. J., 'Planning and Social Life', pp. 134–40.
[2] This is the conclusion arrived at by Gans in his study of the literature on the subject. See Gans, H. J., op. cit.
[3] Kuper, L., op. cit., p. 116.

between people—differences in length of residence, in age, in social status—which work against sociability. But, on the whole, the range of differences among people on the estate—particularly differences in social class, which the other surveys have shown to be so critical—is much narrower than in most districts. In other words, cul-de-sacs and the like *do* help the growth of sociability at Dagenham just because, in the main, the people living nearby are socially not very different from each other.

Differences in age or length of residence may still separate people. But my impression is that, in the cul-de-sacs and similar streets, divisions of this kind are often overcome. Most of the examples, cited earlier, of tensions between old tenants and new came, in fact, from people living in more spread-out roads. New-comers who said they had found their neighbours friendly when they arrived often seemed to be living in the 'banjos' or 'turnings'. Mrs. Farley, who had been living there since 1938, remarked, 'Everyone gets on very well in this banjo. It doesn't matter whether they've been here for a long time or only for two or three years. Everybody treats everybody else in a friendly way.' Mrs. Dover, another woman in a 'banjo', said, 'If anyone new moves in, we always make them welcome. They're all friendly people here, new and old. They showed that by how they helped out when my husband was on strike.'

This chapter began with a question—what accounts for the very different views that people hold of their neighbours, and of the 'matiness' or otherwise of their street? I have suggested a number of answers—differences in the length of time people have lived there, differences in people's ages, differences in social status, and finally differences in street design. Although it is obviously difficult to tease out the relative importance of these various influences, my conclusion is that the last, in the setting of this relatively homogeneous community, is the major determinant.

Thus, the study of patterns of neighbourliness at Dagenham suggests a similar conclusion to that about patterns of kinship. A set of relationships very similar to that of the traditional East End community has developed for some people on the estate, but not for others. With kinship, one reason for the difference is to be found in the management and early planning of the estate, which between them bring in new immigrants and drive away even greater numbers of Dagenham's sons and daughters. With neighbours, the main reason for the difference lies, it seems to me, in the physical design of the estate. What has happened is that, given time and given a working-class population, the familiar patterns have flourished in certain kinds of streets—ones which have something of the physical form of the old East End 'turnings'.

The differences, of course, between Dagenham's 'banjos' on the one hand and Bethnal Green's 'turnings' on the other are still great. The former are built to lower densities than the latter. But they are enough alike nevertheless, because of the physical arrangement of the houses, to allow the development of the traditional ways. If my interpretation is correct, were it not for the spread-out character of so much of the estate's housing, there would be even closer similarities between the social life of Dagenham and of the East End.

VIII

PUBLIC AND PRIVATE LIVING

I HAVE so far looked at social relationships only within a limited range—first with relatives, secondly with non-relatives who visit in the home, and thirdly with other people living nearby. The question still to be answered is how far other kinds of social contacts outside the home supplement these or take their place. What about clubs and societies, for instance? Do these flourish on the estate?

In general, as a number of studies have shown, working-class people tend to belong to such organizations much less than middle-class, and to be much less active in them when they do belong.[1] The middle classes, and especially, it seems, those who live in the suburbs, use these forms of 'organized sociability' partly in order to make up for the fact that they have less to do with relatives or neighbours. What might have happened at Dagenham is that the people there who are isolated from relatives or have only 'distant' relationships with most of their neighbours might follow this example of other suburbanites. But do they?

Societies and organizations have grown up in a place with the population of a large town, as might be expected, ranging from the Dagenham Girl Pipers to the Workers' Educational Association, from the Co-operative Women's Guild to the Dagenham Choral Society. And some of the people we interviewed were members of organizations of this kind. Mr. and Mrs. Ball joined 'the Conservative Club

[1] This has been shown in Derby (Cauter, T., and Downham, J. S., *The Communication of Ideas*, p. 66), in Banbury (Stacey, M., op. cit., p. 69 and p. 81), and in a county town in the Home Counties (Bottomore, T., 'Social Stratification in Voluntary Organisations', pp. 356–82). Also in Woodford (*Family and Class in a London Suburb*, pp. 91–95).

and the British Legion when we arrived here'. Mr. and Mrs. Pink are 'members of the Becontree Social Club and we go along to the Saturday-evening dances. We've got lots of friends there. It's very lively.' Mr. Williams said, 'I belong to the Camera Club and the Tropical Fish Society. As a matter of fact, one of my friends called with his fish last night.'

Dagenham is in line with other places in one respect— white-collar people on the estate seem rather more active in clubs and societies than working-class. But very few of either belong to clubs, as Table 9 shows.

TABLE 9

CLUB MEMBERSHIP AND ATTENDANCE,
ACCORDING TO SOCIAL CLASS

(General sample)

	White Collar	*Working Class*
Attended at least one club or organization within previous month	16%	11%
Not attended within previous month, but member of at least one club or organization	7%	5%
Not member of any club or organization	77%	84%
Total %	100%	100%
Number	94	696

Compared with the middle-class suburb of Woodford, clubs and the like play a small part in people's lives at Dagenham. About half the people in Woodford belong to clubs or associations, compared with only a fifth on the estate, and, though part of Dagenham's difference is due to the difference in its class composition, by no means all of it is. In the private suburb, a third even of working-class people were club members, compared with under a fifth of the working-class people at Dagenham.[1] And there is no indication that the people at Dagenham who have less visits from relatives or friends are any more likely to belong to clubs instead.[2] Such organizations do not, in other words, seem to act as 'substitute' channels for sociability.

It seems unlikely, however, that formal organizations are much more popular in the older working-class communities than they are on the estate. Unfortunately, there is no directly comparable information for Bethnal Green or a similar East End district, though some limited evidence on old people's membership of clubs (of all kinds, not just 'old people's clubs') in Bethnal Green does support this interpretation.[3] The conclusion I would draw, therefore, is that, in terms of club membership and attendance, the estate is less different from the 'traditional' communities than it is from 'middle-class' suburbs.

It is much the same story with churchgoing. Only a tenth of the people in the general sample at Dagenham had been to church in the previous month, and as many as four-fifths said they never went. This is a good deal less than in Woodford.[4] There the middle classes were more often churchgoers, but even working-class people went more than at Dagenham; (57% of working-class people in Woodford said they never went to church, compared with 83% of the working-class majority in Dagenham). But, again, the limited evidence available for Bethnal Green supports my impression that the difference between it and Dagenham is much less sharp.[5]

---

[1] See Table 28 in Appendix 2, which compares both classes in both districts.

[2] See Tables 26 and 27, in Appendix 2.

[3] A survey of 203 old people in Bethnal Green found that 24% belonged to clubs or societies. Townsend, P., *The Family Life of Old People*, pp. 125–6. The proportion of people of similar ages (60 and over for women, 65 and over for men) who did so at Dagenham was 15%.

[4] For a detailed comparison between the churchgoing of middle- and working-class people in both Dagenham and Woodford, see Table 29, in Appendix 2.

[5] Townsend reported that 13% of the old people he interviewed went to church 'as much as once a month' (Townsend, P., op. cit., p. 124); in Dagenham, 9% of people of similar ages said they had been in the previous month.

The absence of 'locals'

Where there is a striking contrast with the older districts is in contacts made in public places. In public houses, for example. They are not much more popular on the estate than churches or clubs—only 21% of the people in the general sample said they had been to a pub during the previous month, and as many as 66% said they never went. As might be expected, men go to pubs more than women—28% of the former had been in the previous month, against 14% of the latter—but most stay away. This was supported by what people in the marriage sample told us. Mr. Hayward said, 'I go out on Saturday night with my friend across the road for a game of darts and a pint.' But only three others of the 50 husbands in the marriage sample said they went out regularly for a drink with friends.

Less people go to pubs on the estate even than in middle-class Woodford,[1] and many less than in the East End. In fact, there are relatively few pubs on the estate. Bethnal Green has a pub for every 600 people, Woodford one for every 2,500, Dagenham one for every 10,000.

It is not only the small number of pubs on the estate—or to put the same point another way, the distances people have to go to get to them—that deter them. The character of the pubs themselves is uninviting. They are mostly vast and cavernous—'about as charming as an aircraft hangar', as one man said—with none of the squashed-up intimacy of an East End bar.

'They did it all wrong when they built those places,' said Mr. Kemp. 'Instead of little pubs that could be like little clubs for the people round about, like they are in Poplar, they built them whacking big places.'

Or as Mr. Andrews said:

'The public houses in Bethnal Green where we used to live were very friendly, small places. When you went up to the bar

---

[1] For a detailed comparison between Dagenham and Woodford, according to social class, see Table 30, in Appendix 2.

you said, "Good evening, Fred, the usual", and you got a "Good evening" reply. But round here you lose the personal touch as far as the pub is concerned. You're just a customer in a big store, sort of thing. They accommodate more people than the pubs in Bethnal Green, and naturally the fewer people there are in a public house the more you know, the more there are the fewer you know.'[1]

There is a similar contrast with shops. The estate now has just over 400 of them—something like one for every 200 people. In Bethnal Green there is one for every 48. Such shops as there are at Dagenham, what is more, are all set in groups around major road junctions—there are no local corner shops, and virtually all are 'lock-up' shops, dead and empty after closing time. This is very different from Bethnal Green, where so many small general shops are part of the shopkeeper's own home. In the East End, as elsewhere, these shops, like the pubs, act as 'social centres'.[2]

The absence of these corner shops might matter less if the estate had a thriving shopping centre, or a street market. People would stand a chance of seeing others they knew there. But these, too, are absent. Mrs. Rank said, 'They haven't got a proper shopping centre here,' and Mr. Pink remarked, 'At the moment if you want anything except the groceries you've more or less got to go to Ilford or Romford.'

Then there is the fact that everything—pub, club, church, fish-shop—is likely to be farther away from the home than in the East End, not only because there are less of them in relation to people, but also because the people they have to serve are so liberally spaced out. 'In Shoreditch,' said Mrs.

---

[1] Jennings has shown that the public houses in Bristol's Barton Hill play the same sort of part in people's lives as they do in the East End. See Jennings, H., op. cit., p. 49.

[2] See Jennings, H., op. cit., pp. 47–48, for a description of the functions of corner shops in Barton Hill, Bristol. Mogey, also, draws the contrast between St. Ebbe's, in Central Oxford, and the suburban housing estate. 'In St. Ebbe's . . . there are regular points where housewives and others meet and exchange information. There was the corner shop . . . the fish-parlour, the café . . . and the various public houses.' Mogey, J. M., op. cit., p. 87.

Gibson, 'everything was handy. Here you've got to walk miles if you want anything.'

There is thus a whole series of ways in which the estate is physically different from the East End communities. The net result is that people at Dagenham lack some of the social opportunities of residents in the older districts. The latter have many more chances—in the immediate locality and rather further afield—for meeting other people informally, and, by this means, for making or renewing acquaintance-ships. This links with the suggestions in the previous chapter about the influence of street layout. It seems clear that the sheer physical anatomy of the old East End community—the short terraced streets built to high density, the corner shops and local pubs, the street markets—is part of the reason for its social character, and that the difference in the life of Dagenham is largely the difference in the way the place is built.

Dagenham has more of the physical environment of a strung-out suburb. But, and this is an important point, the people have not adopted the patterns of middle-class suburbanites. If distances are greater, the pubs and clubs farther away, people have not responded by making the longer journeys that are necessary if one is to reach them. This is partly a practical matter. Less people in Dagenham have their own cars—20% had them in 1958, against 45% in Woodford[1]—and as Mr. Rust said, 'When you get home from work at night, you don't feel like getting changed and walking out to the bus-stop to wait for a bus before you can go to a pub or social club or somewhere like that.' Whatever the reason, clubs, churches and public houses alike all get a good deal less custom than they do in a middle-class suburb like Woodford. In the absence of the locally based institutions of the older community, the people of Dagenham, when they are not at work, have in the main opted to stay at home.

[1] This is, in both districts, the proportion of people in the general sample whose household had a car.

Homes and gardens

The chapter has shown so far that there is relatively little going on in public places at Dagenham. The house is, therefore, more important in people's lives than in the older communities. 'Here you're mostly at home,' said Mr. Hodgson, 'in the evenings and at the week-ends. Hardly anyone goes out except for a special purpose.' There is, of course, nothing at all unusual about this. It is what one might expect to find, above all in a place which is not called a *housing* estate for nothing.

Houses also mean gardens. People were asked what they used their gardens for, and what they felt about them. In addition, a systematic survey of the contents and condition of the *front* gardens of the people in the marriage and tenants' samples was carried out. Judging from people's remarks and what their front gardens looked like, only about a third of those in the marriage sample were enthusiastic gardeners. This almost certainly varies with age—rather more of the people in the tenants' sample, who were mostly in their fifties and sixties, were keen gardeners.[1] But amongst the bulk of those with young children, and many of the older people, too, the garden was mainly used for hanging out washing, for children's play, for storing bicycles, prams and, at the front, even motor-bikes and cars. Most of the people who did 'gardening' aimed not for the kind of display that demanded constant effort and care, but rather for an easily managed tidiness.

'We don't make so much of the garden that it's hard work,' said Mr. Kemp. 'We're not interested in gardening really. We just like to keep the back and front tidy,' said Mrs. Bradshaw. The same attitude was expressed by many of the people whose main interest was in vegetables. 'We don't do much in the garden. I just grow about a dozen

[1] A study of gardening in two middle-class suburbs in Chicago, drawing attention to the fact that some people are 'gardeners' while others are not, also found that older people tended to be more enthusiastic than young. Meyersohn, R., and Jackson, R., 'Gardening in Suburbia', p. 279.

tomato plants every year.' 'We try to do the best we can with it; we grow vegetables in the back.' 'My husband does the garden. Mind you, he doesn't like doing it—he does it to get the benefit of it—with the vegetables.'

The most popular flowers, at least in front gardens, are perennials such as irises, chrysanthemums and michaelmas daisies, hardy plants able to survive in some fashion with very little care. The only common 'improvement' to be seen in front gardens is a concrete path, or a surround, both of which serve the ends of orderliness and, by making flower-beds smaller, of economy. There are naturally wide variations. Something like a fifth of the people in the marriage sample, for example, expressed views like Mr. Roberts, who said he took 'no interest in the garden', or like Mr. Davies, who had 'more or less given it up'. And, at the other extreme, there were great enthusiasts.

> 'That garden's his life,' said Mrs. Hodgson of her husband. 'We have apples and pears and we go in for dahlias a lot. Like last week, all week he was clearing up in the garden and putting in the dahlias. Whenever he can get out there he will; after being at Ford's all day he likes to get out into the air.'

Mr. Williams had 'put in over a hundred rose-bushes, front and back'. Mr. and Mrs. Hayward, who grew 'dozens of flowers'—carnations, dahlias, snapdragons and asters—amidst ornamental trees of laburnum and lilac, also cultivated an allotment.

But apart from exceptional people like these—who seem, as I have said, to be rather more common amongst the older people, though not the very old—most of those at Dagenham, while they use and appreciate their gardens, do not devote all that much attention or effort to them. Though a specific question was not asked, my own impression is that many would be content with smaller gardens, if they were more private, with higher fences or walls, than they are now.[1]

---

[1] A third of the people interviewed in the new town of Stevenage said they would prefer a shorter garden, but with greater privacy, to their present one. See 'Housing Density and Town Design in a New Town', pp. 120–21.

'Do it yourself'

What about the inside of the home? Is the boom in home-decorating and improvement, noted in private suburbs, confined to people who own their own property and can see the point in improving it, or does it extend also to the council tenants of estates like Dagenham? The answer is that enthusiasm for this kind of 'do it yourself' activity seems strong at Dagenham, and much more widespread than for gardening. 'Everybody seems to be a handyman on this estate,' said one man. Another remarked, 'Down here a man makes an art of having something to do in his home when he gets back from work. He realizes he can do things he never thought he could do before.'

The L.C.C.'s maintenance staff redecorates each house, inside and out, every five years. Since 1948 it has also been engaged on a steady programme of modernization—with the tenants' consent, and in return for a weekly addition to the rent, modern tiled grates can be fitted in place of the old, and gas and electric water heaters installed. Many husbands want to go much farther, or are critical of the Council's taste, and although permission has to be sought for major alterations, the L.C.C. does not usually interfere with them.

'The L.C.C.'s wallpapers,' said Mr. Barber, 'are very antiquated, out of this world. Myself I like something pretty modernistic, keeping up with the times. Besides, I re-decorate the place once a year at least.' Mr. Wright said, 'The L.C.C. never comes in here. I do all my own decorating and I prefer it that way. I don't like the way they do it.' His wallpaper is a grey, yellow and blue patterned one on three walls, contrasted with a red and white check on the fourth, the woodwork painted in grey, with red plastic handles and finger panels on the doors. Many people seem to favour so-called 'contemporary' decorations. 'We thought we'd try going contemporary this time,' said Mr. Dover, whose living-room has a yellow, grey and white patterned

92

wallpaper on three walls and another, simulating portland stone, on the fourth, above and around the fireplace. Wallpapers which imitate bricks or stonework seem highly popular in living-rooms, despite the efforts often made to conceal the real brickwork exposed on kitchen walls.

Other people have put in modern equipment like water heaters and new tiled fireplaces, or had them fitted for them. 'We bought that new fireplace,' said one husband. 'The L.C.C. had it put in for us, but we paid, and then I decorated the room.' 'We've put in a lot of things,' said another; 'a better sink, a Sadia electric heater, hot and cold taps.' And a third explained, 'I bought the two Ascots myself—one in the bathroom and one in the kitchen. I'm just putting up a contemporary light fitting in the front room.'

There are other 'improvements' that people have made. In many houses the internal doors have been made 'flush-fitting' with hardboard, painted in lilac or dove grey or covered with 'grained' paper, and fitted with chromium or coloured 'streamlined' plastic handles and ball-catches— 'it's more modern', as one husband explained, 'you just have to push or pull, you see. No old-fashioned handles to turn.' The stair banisters have often been 'boxed-in' with hardboard; so, too, have baths, and simulated tiling (again a form of hardboard) is frequently used in bathrooms and kitchens. 'The L.C.C. just leaves the painted brickwork out here in the kitchen,' said Mr. Mitchell; 'that's not very nice, so we've put this green Congowall all round the side— lots of people put that up—and then painted all the rest with this mimosa gloss paint. With that collapsible table I built myself and these stools, it means we can eat out here in comfort now.' Mr. Andrews had also transformed his kitchen: 'I've papered over the brick walls, giving quite a good effect, and I've removed the old kitchen sink and put in a sink unit. Also a flat-top refrigerator and a flat-top washing machine—that's additional working space, and a very up-to-date kitchen sink. And tables and chairs, where we can have our meals, so that we don't have any meals in the living-room or the front room. We have all our meals entirely in, as we now call it, the kitchenette.'

Furnishings often reflect the same attention to the home. Mr. and Mrs. Salmon, for instance, who have decorated their living-room with a new black and red wallpaper and grey-painted woodwork, have long black folk-weave curtains patterned with flecks of red and blue, a thick fitted carpet in black, red and white, and a three-piece suite in 'charcoal grey uncut moquette', as Mr. Salmon explained, 'from a big store in Ilford'. A 19-inch console television set stands in the corner, its glossy doors closed when it is not in use. There are four black-legged chairs with red plastic seats, a low coffee-table with a cigarette box that plays 'Come back to Sorrento', and a cocktail cabinet whose pink wine glasses are illuminated when the doors open. On the walls are some plaster figures—a fox's head each side of the fireplace, four ducks in flight on one wall and three on another, and a large plaster sun hat on the fourth.

It should not be thought that all homes at Dagenham are so well furnished. The estate has its share of poorer families, and plaster ducks and poverty do not go together. Some people have jobs with relatively low wages, or large families, or both. Others are poor because they are disabled, or widowed, or—among the retired people—because they have only their pension.

About a quarter of the couples in the marriage sample— on the whole where the husbands have unskilled jobs and lower incomes—live in homes more like that of Mr. and Mrs. Davies. Their living-room has no carpet, only a grey and green linoleum whose pattern has been worn away near the fireplace and the door; the wallpaper and woodwork are drab and stained; the only furniture a bare table, a brown leatherette settee, and matching chairs, both worn on the arms, and a television set—the newest and shiniest item in the room. Many of the old people in the tenants' sample, too, had worn and threadbare mats, thin linoleum, grey stuffing peeping from the edges of leatherette chairs and sofas, discoloured wallpaper and fingermarked doors. But the old are not in a majority. The majority, certainly among the younger couples, have homes which reflect both their increased prosperity and their desire to use it in ways that make the family's immediate environment more colourful, more up to date and more comfortable.

IX

AFFLUENCE, STATUS AND CLASS

FOR every Mr. Andrews who already has a 'flat-top refrigerator and washing machine', and every Mr. Salmon who has a suite in 'uncut moquette', there are a dozen others at Dagenham who want the same. 'We're going to do this room up with all new furniture,' said Mrs. Steel. 'My daughters say we're too old-fashioned, so we're going to get something fancy, some of those things with long spiky legs and a sofa off the ground, instead of this old leather.' 'We've seen those new twin-tub washing machines on the telly,' said Mrs. Mitchell, 'I've set my heart on one and we're saving up to put down the deposit.' 'In a place like this, with the shops so far off,' Mr. Wright said, 'you really need a 'fridge. Then the wife could do the shopping all in one go and it would keep fresh, instead of keep going to and fro. That's what we want next.' 'He wants to get a tape-recorder,' Mrs. Dover said, 'but I say an electric sewing machine is more important—for the kiddies' clothes, you know.'

We did not ask people, systematically, which of these various durable goods they owned—only about television, telephone and car. In 1958 over four-fifths of the general sample lived in households with television sets. The few who did not have them were mainly older people and lower-paid couples with large families of dependent children. Only a tenth of the sample, incidentally, had telephones, and hardly any others seemed at all interested in getting one. Cars were different; only a fifth had one, but others hoped to become car-owners in the near future. 'I must admit,' said Mr. Gray, 'a car's very useful in an estate like this.

Next year perhaps we'll be able to manage that.' 'I'd like to get a little car,' said Mr. Bedford, 'It would be nice to take the wife and children out for a run at the week-ends. We're putting so much a week in the Post Office, to tell you the truth, towards the deposit. It doesn't have to be a new one, just something to get the family about in.'

Television sets apart, working-class families in the country as a whole are still far behind middle-class in their ownership of cars and of household durables like refrigerators and washing machines.[1] They exist at Dagenham, as far as I could judge, in nothing like the profusion that even some informants there thought—'Every other house seems to have a washing machine on this estate now,' said Mr. Pink, and Mr. Bradshaw remarked, 'Most people at Dagenham seem to have cars. They're all out there on a Sunday polishing them up, repairing them, talking cars to each other for hours on end.' But, if these views are exaggerated, ownership of cars and household durable goods is certainly spreading. Of still greater importance is the fact that more and more people, even those who own comparatively little themselves, are now aware that what used to be regarded as symbols of middle-class life are no longer so remote. 'Middle-class' standards of consumption are now, in some respects at least, seen as potentially within their grasp.

What is the effect of this awareness upon people's attitudes to each other? Do they strive to outdo their fellows? Are relationships strained and uneasy in consequence? The evidence presented in earlier chapters does not suggest that this happens at Dagenham to any great extent, but the question needs to be examined explicitly.

[1] A national survey by Abrams in 1960 suggested that 52% of middle-class people had a car, against 22% of working-class; 39% against 13% had a refrigerator; 50% against 37% had a washing machine. Television sets were owned by 83% in the middle class, 78% in the working class. (The 'middle class' was defined as 'the one-third of all British families where the chief earner is in a white-collar post and earning at least £800 a year', the 'working class' as the 'remaining two-thirds'.) Abrams, M., 'Bringing Affluence Home', *The Observer*, 23 October, 1960.

'Keeping up with the Joneses'

Informants were asked if they thought there was any tendency for people on the estate to compete with each other in ways like this. Some certainly believed there was.

'One or two people round here will break their necks to keep up with the Joneses. On this estate it's "I've got this and you ain't got that".'

'There are some who talk about their houses more than others. You hear them talking about their 'fridges and washing machines and that. The boastful type, we call them—the type who say, "I'm better than you".'

We discussed this with the 50 couples in the marriage sample; but there were only 13 in which husband or wife or both voiced a complaint of this type. The critics included, first of all, some people who had moved to the estate recently—within the last five years or so—and who felt they and their homes were being judged by their neighbours on their success or failure in meeting Dagenham's standards. One of the women quoted above, who had been a tenant for three years when she was interviewed, said:

'It's awful when they look right through you, because they think you're not as good as them. It isn't "Who are you?" like it is in Bow; it's "What have you got?" '

The other people who complained about rivalry among tenants seemed to come from those with lower incomes and larger families. 'There's a lot of that boasting goes on,' a labourer said, 'One of them will say they've got a new carpet, and if it's not a new carpet it's a washing machine. But I tell my wife, we'll get these things when we come to them.' Sometimes resentment was directed at the fortunate families with more than one wage-earner. 'You get these families,' said a postman, 'where they've got a couple of grown-up children who go out to work. They've got pots of money coming into the home—£50 or £60 a week sometimes. They're the ones who're inclined to be boastful and copy each other.' And another man said, 'You get some people, as soon as someone else has got something they've got to get it as well. We're not like that, though. That mostly happens between people where the husband and wife both go out to work. The things they get—washing machines, 'fridges, cars, the lot!'

But despite these strains—on some of the newer tenants and some of the poorer ones—the overwhelming impression from the interviews is that the improvement in material standards has generated very little tension or anxiety. The majority of those we talked to saw what was happening in a very different way.

'From a working-class point of view, people now have a tendency to reach up. In the past, their houses were spotless, but they never had much furniture. Nowadays they all have good furniture around here. There's more pride—when you buy something now, you go out to buy the real thing. But that's not because of the green-eyed monster, or keeping up with the Joneses. It's because we're all reaching up for the same sort of thing at the same time.'

'People are not so much trying to keep up with each other. They're just striving, all of them, for a higher level.'

'These things like washing machines have become necessities for working-class people. It's not a matter of copying other people. It's everybody wants them when they can get them.'

In this situation, as people explained it, those who were ahead of their neighbours were not so much to be envied as congratulated. 'There's not a bit of jealousy about these things, as far as I can see from people round here,' said one wife, 'People seem to be glad if someone else gets something. They don't grudge it. They say, "Good luck to them".' 'I've never come across any bad feeling,' another said, 'People seem to be only too pleased to think you've got something.'

According to some, the process by which one family

followed another's example was the result of friendly
endorsement rather than rivalry—'People sort of prompt
each other,' as one woman said.

> 'Things become popular among the people you know. You
> see a TV someone's got and you think it would be nice to have
> one like it. Or someone will get a new washing machine and
> they'll show it to you and say how good it is and how much of
> a help to them. It's not envy or anything, it's just recommenda-
> tion. And if you don't get the same thing, they often share
> it with you. The woman next door has got a spin drier, for
> instance. She comes in and takes my washing for me two or
> three times a week and dries it. She does several people's
> drying round here.'

> 'If people buy the same thing it's a compliment more than
> anything. You could call it keeping up with the Joneses, I
> suppose, but it's not really that, it's just because people think
> it's nice. The lady next door says, "Come and see this", and if
> you like it you get one as well.'

Mrs. Wright gave an example:

> 'I was telling the young woman over the road about the
> Marley tiles my husband had just put down in the scullery.
> She seemed interested, so I said, "Why don't you come over
> and look at it?" Now she's seen it she'll tell her husband about
> it. I gave her a sample, as a matter of fact. I expect her husband
> will put some down for her in their scullery. We don't mind
> about that. Why should we?'

Thus in the main people on the estate seem to see their
fellows not as adversaries but as allies in a general advance.
One cannot, of course, rely entirely on what people say
about this kind of thing. One does not know how far they
are misleading themselves about what is really happening.
But, to the outsider, competition between neighbours certainly seems less keen, anxiety over possessions less sharp,
at Dagenham than elsewhere; in the private suburb of
Woodford, for example, or in the new estate of Greenleigh.
There is little sign of 'status striving'.

What social class?

One reason for this relative harmony, as some people on the estate saw it, is that by and large the residents are similar kinds of people.

'The people here, they're the same as us, and we're the same as them. None of us are rich people. They're not snobbish, because it's a working-class district, isn't it, really?'
'It's all working class here. We've all moved in together; we've all come from working-class families, and people brought up like that understand one another.'

This sense of social solidarity seems to be reinforced by the immense size of the place. So large is it, in both area and population, that it constitutes a vast one-class township. It is big enough to have an identity of its own, and not to be 'overawed' by neighbouring districts. Unlike the manual workers at Woodford, who are surrounded by—and judged deficient by—the suburb's usual models of behaviour, most of the residents of Dagenham are insulated, by the size and location of the estate, from middle-class influences. Many who work at Ford's or one of the other local factories and live on the estate seldom venture outside the area from one week to the next. Even the District Line railway which serves the estate, helps to support this detachment; from the East End through to Dagenham itself, it passes exclusively through working-class East London. Unlike most other suburban lines, it carries relatively few clerks or managers—only those who go past Dagenham to Upminster, where, as a railway worker said, 'You do get some of the types who think they're superior—bowler hats, and sandwiches in their briefcases. But there aren't many like that on this line.'

Nor do people from Ilford or Romford, to the north, exert much influence on the life of the estate. Some people were aware, as one man put it, that 'they rather look down on Dagenham because it's a council estate'. Another said, 'The people in Ilford loathe Dagenham—they'd wipe it out if they could. They call it corned-beef city.' One wife countered by saying, 'In Ilford they're all fur coats and no drawers', and another—'They're all show and no breakfast.' It may be significant that these complaints came from people living near to the Ilford borders of the estate. On the whole Dagenham residents seemed hardly aware of the different standards of those other districts, or indifferent to them; they certainly did not seem to feel oppressed by them.

This was reflected in people's answers when they were asked what social class they thought they belonged to, as distinct from the class into which they had been assigned according to their, or their husband's, jobs. They were put a completely 'open' question, without any alternative answers being offered.[1] Only 13% of the people who were working class in occupation described themselves as 'middle class'. As might be expected, more white-collar people said they were 'middle class': 27% did so, though more even of them (39%) said 'working class' instead.

The proportion of people with manual jobs describing themselves as 'middle class' at Dagenham was lower than in other districts where the question has been put. In Greenwich the proportion was 23%; in Hertford, 31%; in Woodford, 34%.[2] The higher the proportion of manual workers in the area, the lower the proportion who assign themselves to the 'middle class'.

By no means all the rest of the working-class people at Dagenham described themselves as 'working class': 54% did so, leaving 33% who did not assign themselves to any social class at all. These last divided evenly between those

[1] Only a tiny minority of people at Dagenham answered our 'open' question with such terms as 'lower middle', 'upper working', 'lower' and so on. Of the few who did, those who said they were 'lower middle' and the like were put with those saying 'middle class', the others with those saying 'working'.

[2] The figures for Greenwich and Hertford, where as in Dagenham an 'open' question was put, have been calculated from Table 4 on p. 56 of Martin, F. M. 'Some Subjective Aspects of Social Stratification.' That from Woodford from our general survey there. In Woodford people were asked the question in two forms. The first was 'open'—to which 34% of working-class people said 'middle class'. The second offered a list of 'classes' for people to choose from; this time the proportion saying 'middle' or 'lower middle class' went up to 48%.

who gave some other answer and those who gave none at all. Many stressed their own 'ordinariness'—'We're nothing out of the ordinary', 'Average—same as everyone else', 'Just ordinary folk', 'We're ordinary everyday types'. Others denied the existence of class—'Social class is just a television cliché', 'I don't think there are really any classes' —and others gave various answers which suggested that 'class' meant something quite different to them. 'We're sociable with everybody,' they said. Or, 'We mix in with everybody round here', 'Not well off, we just get along', 'We don't belong to anything', 'Good Christian people'. Finally, there were those who said they were unable to answer the question; most of their comments showed that concepts of class did not figure much in their thoughts either—'I don't know what you mean', 'I've never thought about it', 'I don't know much about it'.

I do not want to oversimplify, because this whole question of class identification is obviously complex and elusive. Different people do not necessarily mean the same things by terms like 'working class' or 'middle class', and indeed the same person may at different times or in different contexts use them in different senses and locate himself differently.[1] The index used—people's responses to one standardized question—is in any case a very limited and crude guide to what they really think. But the present evidence suggests that people on this estate neither regard themselves as 'middle class' in very large numbers nor are very concerned about what social class they might belong to.

Political loyalties

This chapter seems to indicate so far that, despite people's interest in their homes and desire for material advancement, their attitudes to each other and their views of social class are probably not very different from those in the old working-class districts. In politics the districts are

[1] This is discussed in Martin, F. M., op. cit. The extent to which different sorts of people use social class concepts, and the different 'models' of class that may be used, are discussed by Bott, E., *Family and Social Networks*, Chapter VI.

undoubtedly alike. The constituency (which is coterminous with the borough of Dagenham, not the L.C.C. estate) is as overwhelmingly Labour as is Bethnal Green. It has had a Labour council ever since it became a borough, and in parliamentary elections it boasts one of the largest Labour majorities in the country.[1]

We discussed their political opinions with the 50 men in the marriage sample. Unfortunately, I can say nothing about the views of their wives, for these questions were specifically addressed to the men. The reader should bear in mind that women are less likely to describe themselves as 'working class' than men—at Dagenham 47% of the wives of manual workers, against 59% of men with manual jobs said they were 'working class'—and are also less likely to vote Labour.[2] The great majority of the men—44 out of the 50 —had voted Labour at the previous election in 1955, and with the exception of three who said they would give their vote to the Liberals or Communists if they had the chance, all firmly intended to vote Labour again, at the next election (in 1959). The minority—three Conservatives and three who did not vote—are too few for any generalization, so what I have to report is from the remarks of these Labour supporters.

They were asked their reasons for favouring Labour. A few spoke about political ideals. 'Labour is socialist,' said one. 'It stands for equality, a fair deal for everyone.' 'Socialism,' said another, 'means being friendly with everyone. I think that's right. You've got to apply that everywhere, all over the world, and that's what Labour stands for.' And a third explained, 'Labour is closer to Christianity, to my way of thinking, than the Conservatives are.'

A much more common reason given for voting Labour

[1] Moser, C. A., and Scott, W., *British Towns*, show that in the 1951 General Election Dagenham had the fourth highest 'Left vote' (76.1%) of all the 157 English and Welsh 'towns' studied; and the 1955 the third highest (73.9%), p. 118.

[2] See, for example, Benney, M., Gray, A. P., and Pear, R. H., *How People Vote*, p. 107; Milne, R. S., and Mackenzie, H. C., *Marginal Seat*, p. 60; Lipset, S. M., *Political Man*, p. 231.

was that it was the party that represented the interests of the working class—four-fifths of the Labour supporters stressed this. The reader may wonder how this links with what was said earlier about people's subjective views about their social class membership. Of the 41 'Labour supporters' (that is, the men who had both voted Labour in 1955 and said firmly that they intended to do so again in 1959), 33 gave a reason along the lines that the Labour Party 'stands for the working class'. Together with the one Communist, who was 'militantly' working class, this means that 34 men of the sample of 50—or 68%—obviously regarded themselves as in some sense 'working class'. It may seem on the face of it difficult to reconcile this with the 59% of manual-class men in the general sample (57% of men in the sample altogether, including the white-collar workers) who, in answer to our question about class, said they were 'working class'. The explanation is partly that there were a few men who, in the context of that question, did not think of themselves as 'working class', but who did in terms of politics. They had said they 'didn't know' what class they belonged to when interviewed in the general survey, and later, when talking about politics, made statements like 'being working class, of course I'm Labour'. This kind of shift only shows again that people's conceptions of class are far from simple or static. The explanation is partly also that the men in the marriage sample are not typical, in their class identification, of men in the general sample as a whole. There is a tendency for younger men to describe themselves as 'working class' more often, and the men in the marriage sample were younger; among working-class men the proportions in different age groups in the general sample saying they were 'working class' were 20–39, 65%; 40–59, 57%; 60 and over, 55%. It is, incidentally, sometimes suggested that the sense of class solidarity is weaker among younger workers than old;[1] whether or not this applies elsewhere, it does not seem to be true at Dagenham.

[1] Abrams found, in a national sample survey, that more people aged 18 to 24 said

The majority, among the men in the marriage sample, who supported the Labour Party for class reasons expressed it like this:

'I'm a working-class man, so I couldn't vote anything else. Labour stands for the working-class people.'

'Labour is for the ordinary folk, for the working class, and we've grown up with that class of people.'

'I'm a trade unionist. The way I see it, there's only one way for me to vote. I mean, it doesn't make sense to pay your union subs. to one side and then go and vote for the other.'

'I've got nothing to conserve. Labour's the working man's party.'

Many people with views of this sort took little active interest in politics. 'I'm not a political man,' said one man, 'I just vote Labour.' 'We don't go in for politics a lot,' said another, 'We just vote our opinion when it comes along and that's more or less it.' And another, 'I vote Labour because I'm a working man. Apart from that I've never gone into it, to tell you the truth.'

Others were inclined to be cynical, even anarchistic, about politics.

'The top brass of both parties have got very little between them, but I back Labour. I always have.'
'Whether they're Labour or Tory they're both governments, aren't they? But I think the Labour Party might be able to do a little bit more for the working class.'

Not surprisingly perhaps, given such opinions, political interest is at a relatively low level at Dagenham; the proportions voting in general and local elections are among the

---

they were 'middle class' than of those aged 25 or over. But the sample was not large, and nor was the difference—60% of the younger people said they were 'middle class', against 'little more than half' of the older. Abrams, M., and Rose, R., *Must Labour Lose?* p. 53.

lowest in the country.[1] Most men (in the winter of 1958–59) had little idea of Labour's current policy. 'Employment and housing, mainly,' was one answer. 'More or less to do more for the working class, I suppose,' said a lorry driver. 'I don't know exactly what their policy is, to tell you the truth,' another man confessed, 'They're against high rents, aren't they?' Mr. Page was an exception—'They're going to put in a scheme for old people so they've got something more to live on than shirt buttons.' So was Mr. Palmer—'Labour's got this new pension scheme. That's a very good thing. They stand for more social security, better social services.' One item of Labour policy, apart from 'giving a fair deal to the working man', that many people did talk about was nationalization. Some were in favour of it:

'Labour ought to go for more nationalization and do it properly, not like they've done so far. Those shareholders never had a penny from the railways or the mines before the war and now they're getting paid a regular 5%. I'd give them compensation, but it would be a lot less than they've got up to now.'

'I think there should be complete nationalization, because otherwise they won't find the money for this Welfare State. Labour's not Left-wing enough for me. They have very good convictions to begin with, but then they seem to lose them and become sort of Right of Centre.'

But these two were outnumbered by the Labour supporters who took the opposite view.

'I'm Labour, but I don't agree with all this nationalization. Going by my job, nobody cares how the buses are run. You see, there aren't any shareholders to chase people up. You get the couldn't-care-less attitude.'

[1] This, again, is the Borough of Dagenham, not the estate. It should not be assumed that a large majority for one party automatically means a relatively low turn-out (on the grounds, as it were, that the result is a foregone conclusion). The South Wales 'towns' of Rhondda and Merthyr Tydfil had, in 1951 and 1955, the two largest Labour majorities among the 157 English and Welsh towns listed by Moser and Scott; but they also had much higher polls than Dagenham. See Moser, C. A., and Scott, W., op. cit., p. 119 and p. 151.

'I don't like the idea of nationalizing everything. The hospitals and the railways and the mines, yes. But other things, I don't think so. Private enterprise can do the other things better.'

Some Labour voters echoed Conservative criticisms of nationalization. Others, while remaining loyal to their party, seemed to share the Conservatives' view of themselves as the more dynamic and efficient party.

'I agree in principle with the Tory Government about free enterprise, it seems to be a good idea, but I've always voted Labour. I was brought up with Labour. It's your class, isn't it?'

'I don't know much about politics. I vote Labour; I always have. But this Conservative idea of "free enterprise" rather appeals to me.'

Despite a few doubts like this, the general picture is one of solid support for Labour, support based largely upon class interests and loyalties.

This chapter, to conclude, has presented a rather different account of people's behaviour and values from what might have been expected in a housing estate. To be sure, people there have rising standards and aspirations. They want all sorts of things for themselves and their families—better furniture, more labour-saving machinery, cars, electric shavers, hi-fi sets, formica-topped tables, lilac paintwork and the rest. But they do not see their demands for these things as being in rivalry with those of their fellows. At Dagenham, the material prosperity enjoyed in the past decade has not, as far as one can judge, been at the expense of traditional attitudes. Dagenham seems, indeed, to be as predominantly working class a community in sentiment as it is in occupation, and as much so as the East End itself.

X

IN CONCLUSION—THE
WORKING-CLASS COMMUNITY

THROUGHOUT this book Dagenham has been compared with the 'traditional' working-class community. At the end one is impressed by how similar, not how different, they are. Local extended families, which hold such a central place in the older districts, have grown up in almost identical form on the estate, and so have local networks of neighbours—people living in the same street who help each other, mix together and are on easy-going terms. In people's attitudes to their fellows, their feelings about social status and class, their political loyalties, again, there are close parallels between the two districts. In part, Dagenham is the East End reborn.

I must, of course, add the qualifications. It seems clear that the failure to plan for an expanding population—with more homes, and different-sized homes—has, together with a housing administration which denies two-thirds of the vacancies to local people, frustrated the creation of more extended families at Dagenham. It seems clear, from the comparison of different types of street layout, that the spread-out character of many of the roads has worked against the growth of the old style of neighbourliness. It seems clear that the sprawl of the estate as a whole, and the failure to provide a lively civic centre or local corner shops and pubs, have discouraged the development of social mixing, formal or informal.

In these and many other ways, the setting was, and is, one would have thought, extremely unpromising. There were all the initial inadequacies—the lack of local industry, schools, transport and the rest, the 'one age-group' population. And there are the difficulties that remain—the uniformity of architecture; the continued dearth of public buildings, shops and transport;[1] the division of the estate between three local authority areas (which has inhibited any growth of civic feeling about the place as a whole). Given all these discouragements, it seems incredible that people have managed to develop a way of life so much like the old.

It is a way of life, what is more, that satisfies most people. Many of them are not oppressed by the architectural monotony and dreariness which fill the visitor with gloomy amazement that people could live in such a place, let alone enjoy it. The inhabitants express affection for it. Mr. Brooks, a toolmaker in an engineering factory, went to Dagenham when he was 16, and is now 38.

> 'I know Dagenham seems monotonous to people from outside,' he said, 'but when you've been living here a while, the roads develop their own personalities—there are landmarks which you get to recognize in different turnings. Anyway, it's not the outside of the houses that matter, it's what's inside them. I've got a number of good friends here. Lots of the people round here know me. I get on extremely well with the shopkeepers in the district. My roots are here now and I'm very happy indeed.'

Time and again, people said similar things. 'I like the district and I like the neighbours.' 'I like Dagenham, I like it very well.' 'In my opinion it's a nice place to live.' 'I like it here. It's ideal if you're a working man.' To report this contentment is not, of course, to excuse bad architecture or town planning, nor to imply that Dagenham's faults do not matter, rather to draw attention to human resilience and the vitality of traditional social patterns.

---

[1] A study of labour mobility in Dagenham in 1951 reported: 'Interviews with those among the Dagenham workers who were residents of the borough show that the area lacks good shopping facilities, adequate transport and sufficiently varied entertainment.' Jefferys, M., *Mobility in the Labour Market*, p. 29.

This survey suggests that earlier studies of housing estates have put altogether too little emphasis on sheer length of residence. Partly because of this, and partly because so much past writing in sociology has forecast the breakdown of 'traditional' forms of social solidarity,[1] there has been a habit, when discussing the kind of community that has been discovered in the old central areas of our cities, of regarding it as an anachronism, the vestigial remnant of a dying way of life. This is clearly wrong. Although working-class life is obviously changing in many ways—people have more possessions, are more 'home-centred', and, whether they live in the old districts or the new, probably spend more time with their families—there are, apparently, some fundamental regularities in working-class life which, given time, will reassert themselves. It now seems to me that what happens on the new estates is not so much working-class people adopting middle-class ways, as working-class people trying to adapt themselves to a strange new environment. It is striking, on the whole, not only how similar Dagenham's patterns are to those of Bethnal Green, but also how dissimilar they are from those of middle-class suburbia.[2]

There are obviously many people to whom the kind of locally based life that some enjoy at Dagenham does not appeal. There are some residents who are not only rather 'reserved' in their dealings with others, but also say they prefer it that way. 'They're not too friendly,' said one husband, 'and that's how we like it.' And some find the estate *too* sociable compared with other districts. 'It's different here from Hornsey,' said a man who had previously lived there. 'Here they are apt to try to get too close, to pry into your

---

[1] See, e.g., Tönnies, F., *Community and Association*, which distinguished 'Gemeinschaft' (community) and 'Gesellschaft' (association), and saw modern society as abandoning the first kind of grouping in favour of the second.

[2] A recent sociological study of a Californian suburb, largely populated by manual workers and their families, came to a similar conclusion. The author set out to see how far the lives of people there were like those in 'middle-class' suburbs, and he concluded, 'these suburbanites have not, to any marked extent, taken on the patterns of behaviour and belief associated with white-collar suburbs'. Berger, B. M., *Working-Class Suburb*, pp. 92–93.

business. In Hornsey people are more reserved.' Many people, too, have already moved away from the estate, and if in the beginning most did so because Dagenham was too different from their old community, more have done so in recent years—including many members of the estate's second generation—because it was not different enough. But the fact that some people have gone, because they found Dagenham too uniform, too depressing, or too limiting, does not challenge the conclusion that many of those who stay have not only re-created the familiar local ties, but are content to have done so.

*   *   *   *   *

I want, finally, to raise some of the town planning issues suggested by this inquiry, and discuss the implications both for Dagenham and for other communities. First, the question of social class.

Dagenham, like the older districts, is largely one class. It is certain, as an earlier chapter suggested, that neighbourly relationships are more likely to develop in the *street* if people are similar to each other in social background. It seems, too, as if this kind of homogeneity amongst residents has an influence upon the social character of the local community more widely as well, and upon attitudes and relationships within it.[1]

It is easy to see why living in a one-class community might make for relative social harmony. One man had previously lived in Hendon and much preferred Dagenham. 'Hendon was very nice but, realizing that I'm a working man, I'm happier here. I always come back home dirty from work. At Hendon people looked down on you if you had dirty clothes on, but here they take you for granted.'

---

[1] This point is made by Lockwood, D., and Goldthorpe, J. H., in an unpublished paper, 'The Manual Worker: Affluence, Aspirations and Assimilations', pp. 18–23, which contains a scholarly and perceptive discussion of the question of whether the working class is becoming 'bourgeois', and what kinds of influence have a bearing on the process. A shorter, published discussion of the same subject can be found in Lockwood, D., 'The "New Working Class" '.

A woman who works part time as a machine-operator, and whose husband is a building labourer, had been brought up in Epping. 'It's a real Tory place,' she said. 'They seem to be more snobbish there. Mind you, I like the place being as my home was there, but it wasn't as friendly there as it is here.' Dagenham is one of those districts (unlike most suburbs, but like the East End) where the working-class people feel more at home than the middle class.

The views some expressed about the social deviants on the estate are also instructive. Chapter V suggested that many of the emigrants from Dagenham have been white-collar people. Other residents not only recognized that this emigration took place, they welcomed it. 'The first thing the snobs do,' as one man put it, 'is to change their address.' 'There are one or two snobs here,' said another, 'You do meet them. People like that shouldn't be in the estate. They should get out and buy themselves a house, not stay on making other people feel uncomfortable.' This resentment, it should be noted, exactly matches the attitude of some of the middle-class residents of Woodford, who complained that working-class people coming into the district were 'lowering the tone'. In both districts, in other words, some people who belong to the social class in the majority are intolerant of the minority. A whole series of studies have, in fact, shown how widespread is people's desire to live amongst others like themselves.[1]

All this raises an important—and disturbing—question. If most people prefer not to mix with those in other social classes, is what town planners have thought of as one of Dagenham's biggest faults really an asset from the point of view of its residents? The hope behind the 'socially balanced community' is that mixing the classes physically will encourage them to mix socially. As the then Minister of Town and Country Planning expressed it in 1948, discussing the proposed new towns, 'I am very concerned, indeed, not

[1] See, for instance, Hutchinson, B., *Willesden and the New Towns*, p. 40, and Stacey, M., op. cit., p. 115.

merely to get different classes . . . living together in a community, but to get them actually mixing together. . . . Unless they do mix, and mix freely, in their leisure and recreation the whole purpose of . . . a mixed community disappears.'[1]

But it seems that this is unlikely to happen, that to put people together who feel they have nothing in common is more likely to generate social tensions than to reduce them. The contrast between Dagenham, where there is little evidence of tension among the residents, and Woodford, which is a mixed-class district with a good deal of it, suggests this. So does the experience of the new towns so far. 'Most new towns', reports Nicholson, 'now accept, though sometimes with reluctance, that an attempt to promote social mixing by building "managerial" houses scattered throughout the town and its neighbourhoods, without the alternative of such houses built in groups, has failed.'[2] What seems apparent is that this planning theory, which attracted so much support in the 'post-war reconstruction' mood of 1945, is Utopian and naïve. In a society in which social and economic differences divide people as much as they do in Britain, the attempt to bring the different classes together through town planning, by forcing them to be neighbours, is doomed to disappointment.

Disadvantages of a one-class community

On the other hand, there are disadvantages in too great a social uniformity as in too great a diversity. Dagenham bears this out as well.

First, the virtual absence of a middle class on the estate no doubt has something to do with the relative lack of interest of local clubs and organizations, since they are the

---

[1] Silkin, L., 'Housing Layout in Theory and Practice', quoted in Orlans, H., *Stevenage*, p. 82.
[2] Nicholson, J. H., op. cit., p. 132. See also Osborn, F. J., *Green-Belt Cities*, on the experience of the pre-war new towns of Letchworth and Welwyn—'whatever the town planner may desire, people have a marked tendency to segregate themselves by class or income' (p. 93).

kind of people who are so often the initiators and supporters of such forms of activity. Secondly, the estate might be better able to support a thriving shopping centre, with fuller entertainment, cultural and restaurant facilities—it is certainly large enough to justify one—if it had more middle-class customers in the area to draw on.

Thirdly, there is the question of the 'expatriates' of the second generation. Some of those who could afford to do so, or were middle class in occupation or aspiration, moved away not only because homes were scarce on the estate, but also because they could not find houses of the standard or size they wanted, or because they sought the company of people with similar tastes and interests to their own. Had Dagenham been able to offer greater social and architectural variety, some at least of these would have stayed. As one daughter said, 'We didn't want a council house, but if we could have bought the kind of house we wanted in Dagenham we would have stayed there.' People like her would then have been nearer to their parents, nearer to other people they had grown up with, and the estate would surely have gained.

Fourthly, there is no doubt in my mind that education at Dagenham suffers from the estate's social uniformity. Schools in mixed-class districts benefit from the enthusiasm and stimulus of middle-class parents and their children, who help to create an atmosphere which can be stimulating, though it can also produce strains,[1] for the gifted children from working-class homes. As a Dagenham headmaster put it, one of his difficulties was that very few of his children came from homes in which there was 'an appreciation of culture, of the arts', and there was little intellectual or cultural cross-fertilization between children from different kinds of social background.

We talked to the people in the marriage sample about their children's education, and found some support for the view that most parents on the estate are not educationally

[1] See Jackson, B., and Marsden, D., *Education and the Working Class.*

ambitious for their children, and do not take a keen interest in their schooling. A few do. A printer said about his son, 'I'd like him to win a scholarship. He takes the exam. next year. Of course, we don't know whether he'll get it, but we definitely want him to, and will give him every encouragement for his education. I'd like him to go all the way, if he's got the ability, that is.' The other parents seem less enthusiastic:

> 'I've never really thought about it. I've always taken it for granted he'll leave school at 15 unless he turns out brilliant and goes to College.'

> 'I don't care a lot myself. The main thing is for the children to be happy.'

> 'It's immaterial to us. If he wants to go in for the 11-plus, we wouldn't stand in his way.'

It is perhaps not surprising that Moser and Scott showed Dagenham in 1951 to have the third highest proportion (among the 157 'towns' listed) of children leaving school under the age of 15 (84.4%) and the very lowest proportion of people between 15 and 24 in full-time education (3.8%).[1] In part, this is simply a reflection of the class composition of the area, since working-class children in any area are less likely to stay on at school, but I would think the lack of social variety was an additional explanation.

There is a wider issue here as well. The local headmaster quoted earlier also explained that many of his intelligent children found it difficult to stay on into the Sixth Form. The pressures were partly economic, he said, but in addition, 'Some of those who stay on feel they are being isolated from their contemporaries. In some cases they are looked at askance simply because they have different ideas.' This points to another problem of an overwhelming working-class community—that those who grow up in it with in-

---

[1] Moser, C. A., and Scott, W., op. cit., p. 118. Again the area is the borough, not the estate, but I see no reason for thinking that the estate would have a better showing; if anything, since it is rather more uniform, it would probably be worse.

tellectual or cultural talents or interests, or indeed with other kinds of interests which do not fit into the conventional mould, may lack stimulus or encouragement, or may find the pressures to conformity too inhibiting, their opportunities restricted, their life cramped.

Striking a balance

To recapitulate briefly: when people live amongst 'their own kind' they feel socially more at ease than when they are mixed. But, on the other hand, a district or a town which is one class (certainly if it is predominantly working class, or, for that matter, predominantly middle class) is impoverished in some important ways. It looks therefore as if it would be sensible to accept that most people do not want to be too mixed; and to plan for one-class 'neighbourhoods'—but in mixed-class communities.[1] The 'neighbourhoods', which would, of course, only be 'one class' in the sense that their houses would be at similar kinds of rents or prices, would need to be large enough to give the residents a sense of social ease, but not so large (as Dagenham is) that they isolated people from those in other classes; and schools, shops (other than corner shops), cinemas, restaurants, libraries and so on would be sited where they would serve two or more 'neighbourhoods' of differing social composition.

This proposal cuts across the current planning conception of 'neighbourhoods'—'socially mixed' and physically distinct areas of some 5,000–10,000 people—which are the basic units of most of the present new towns. The main purpose of grouping dwellings would not be, as it is at present, to create 'community' in mixed-class 'neighbourhoods', but rather to enable 'community' to develop in one-class 'neighbourhoods', which would be linked to each other through common services. In this way people could

[1] An American sociologist, in a review of the 'balanced community' concept, arrived at similar recommendations—namely, homogeneity at the level of the 'block', heterogeneity at the level of the community. Gans, H. J., 'The Balanced Community—Homogeneity or Heterogeneity in Residential Areas', pp. 180–1.

become aware of the variety of society at large, and of the opportunities open to them, without the strain of adapting to—or conflicting with—neighbours with a different style of life.

This is, at present, no more than a suggestion about a different way of approaching the problem of social class differences in designing, for instance, a new town; many questions remain unanswered. An obvious one is what size the 'neighbourhoods' would need to be—the experience of Woodford suggests a possible minimum population of 1,000 to 2,000 for working-class 'neighbourhoods'.[1] But this, and the many other questions raised, can only be satisfactorily answered by further studies of the experience of different kinds of community in new towns and old. Meanwhile, as for Dagenham itself, there is no doubt in my mind that it is poorer in some ways because of its monolithic social uniformity. One wonders whether, even now, it might not be possible to provide some homes for sale, or at economic rents, on the estate. There would need to be enough of them, again, to avoid their middle-class inhabitants feeling too isolated from the rest of the population. But this is part of the wider question, to which I now turn, of providing more homes for the estate's second generation.

Planning for the second generation

If new communities are to develop into settled ones, there must be an opportunity for people who grow up in them to go on living there if they want to after they marry. People who have grown up in an area know each other, know the district; they feel, as they put it themselves, 'at home' there. Some wish to leave; that is up to them. But the claim of the others to be allowed to go on living in the district seems to me to be strong. And it is not only the emigrants them-

---

[1] The study in Woodford noted the existence of distinct working-class 'enclaves', where people seemed more content than those of their fellows who lived amongst middle-class residents. These 'enclaves' contained something between 1,000 and 2,000 people. *Family and Class in a London Suburb*, pp. 119–20.

selves who are affected. At Dagenham, it is clear, there are some parents on their own whose children would be living near them if they could. One of the disturbing aspects of the Dagenham scene is the growing proportion of old people in the estate's population; in the years ahead there is likely to be an increasing strain upon old people themselves, their neighbours, and the local social services. This would be less of a problem if all the sons and daughters who were ready to stay had been able to do so.

As Chapter IV showed, there are two sets of obstacles. The first result from the failure to provide for the 'natural expansion' of the population that was bound to follow from the unbalanced age structure of the first decade. The obvious solution in new communities is to plan in advance for enough homes—and for homes of differing sizes. Though some suburban housing estates built since 1945 have provided more variety in dwelling-sizes than Dagenham did, few seem to have considered the problems of the second generation. The new towns, on the other hand, are for the most part aware of the need. Basildon, for instance, is building flats for the children of tenants. Harlow, to give another example, is slowing down its home-building until it can gauge its future requirements more accurately. Though the problem is now recognized, however, most new towns did not anticipate it early enough, and to meet it some will have to extend the town's boundaries or to take land planned as open space for housing instead.[1]

The lessons are clear. In any new settlement it is essential, first, to try to attract people of all ages, and, secondly, since even at best it is too much to hope for an age structure like that of a settled town, to prepare in advance for the right kinds of homes in the right places to meet the inevitable increase in population and change in its age structure.[2] Unless houses of the right sort are available for them,

[1] Nicholson, J. H., op. cit., pp. 63–64.
[2] These needs were fully recognized by the L.C.C.'s team working on *The Planning of a New Town*; see pp. 18–20.

children will be forced to move away who would have preferred to stay, while at the same time there will be old people occupying houses larger than they need. At Dagenham, where the estate and the sites around it are now fully built up, this warning comes too late. As we have seen, many children who wanted to stay have already had to go, and yet many houses are 'under-occupied'. But some measures could still be taken. One proposal, which the L.C.C. is looking into, is to convert some of the houses on the estate into flats; if older people would move into these—as some undoubtedly would—this would free larger houses for growing families.[1] Another possibility would be to demolish some houses and build to higher densities on the vacated sites.

More dramatically, the problem—and some others, too—might be met by following the example of the Stockholm suburb of Vallingby and building over the top of the railway line that at present cuts through the estate at the cost of many acres of land. A private scheme for building a department store over the railway at Heathway was in progress when this book went to press; but something much more ambitious might be attempted. A redevelopment scheme, involving the multiple use of land on somewhat similar lines to Vallingby or to the 'Living Suburb' project produced by a group of architects for Ealing's Boston Manor,[2] but putting flats as well as shops, cinemas and restaurants above the railway, could provide Dagenham with an exciting and attractive centre.[3] If, to take up the earlier point, this included some more expensive homes, the estate would get the advantage of greater social variety.

The second obstacle to those of the second generation who wish to stay is the continued use by the L.C.C. of houses falling vacant for new migrants from London. The

---

[1] Such conversions have been carried out on at least one of Bristol's council estates. See 'Southmead Flats for Old Folk', *Bristol Evening World*, 4 September 1958.

[2] Chamberlin, Powell and Bon, Shankland, G. and Jones, D. G., 'The Living Suburb.'

[3] This kind of development would be possible under the Transport Act, 1962.

issue here is how long a local authority which creates a new community outside its own boundaries should continue to control the tenancies there. As long as it does, continuity of residence is frustrated: the place cannot easily develop like any other district where, though there may be migration in and out, there is also a large settled core of people who have been born and grown up in the locality. The estate remains in one sense a transit camp, repopulated in every generation by a new wave of migrants whose own children will be forced in time to move on in their turn.

The problem arises in any new estate of this kind. It was evident at the L.C.C.'s out-County estate at Watling in 1939, where Durant remarked of the children, 'as they get older and marry it is impossible for them to remain here even if they wish. There is hardly any accommodation for childless households and, in any case, they are not eligible as tenants, since, as a rule, the L.C.C. accepts only people from the London Area.'[1] In Bristol's estates likewise:

> 'If Council houses continue to be allocated primarily in connexion with slum clearance and the abatement of overcrowding, relatively few can be let to these newly married couples. Of the couples married at Filwood Church from 1937 to 1939, for example, not one appears to have remained on the estate after marriage. The tendency must be for them to seek accommodation off the estates in houses or, more often, 'rooms' or quasi-flats; these are to be found mainly in the old districts, perhaps in the very areas from which the young couples moved as children.'[2]

Throughout the country the same conflict is, or will be, posed by estates like this. By the L.C.C.'s other 26 out-County estates in Essex, Hertfordshire, Kent and Surrey; by Liverpool's estates at Norris Green and Kirkby; Manchester's at Wythenshawe and Langley; Birmingham's at Kingstanding; by hundreds of others elsewhere. The problem does not arise in the new towns, which control their

---

[1] Durant, R., *Watling*, p. 15.
[2] Jevons, R., and Madge, J., *Housing Estates*, p. 54.

own tenancies, nor in housing estates in 'expanded towns' —under the Town Development Act, the local authorities will in time take these over. Despite the pressing needs of London and the other cities, my own view is that the ownership and control of estates like Dagenham should be passed, on fair terms, to the local councils.[1]

Planning and layout

I will not reiterate in detail all the obvious planning deficiencies of estates like Dagenham. The failure to provide local industry from the beginning; the absence of communal buildings and of adequate transport (both faults from which the estate still suffers); the lack of any centre—all these were recognized long ago, and have partly been remedied in the new towns built since 1945, if not in the recent crop of suburban housing estates. Here the Dagenham survey simply confirms what was already well known.

Some conclusions can be drawn from this study, however, about street layout—and how it can influence the extent to which people have neighbourly relations with each other. It can do so in three main ways. The first is by the physical 'framing' of the housing unit—the street, the 'banjo' or whatever it may be. If this has a clear physical unity, people find it easier to feel a sense of identity with it and with their fellow residents. Secondly, the actual arrangement of the dwellings in relation to each other—and thus to the routes in and out—can have an influence. The 'banjos' provide the most obvious illustration of this at Dagenham. And thirdly, there is the more general issue of housing density. Other things being equal, the closer homes are to each

---

[1] If the Government's proposals for reforming London government go through, the estates will first be taken over by the new Greater London Council. 'But in time', in the words of the Government White Paper, 'all these houses ought, in the Government's opinion, to be transferred to local ownership and management.' *London Government: Government Proposals for Re-organisation*, p. 8. Since the suggestion is that Dagenham and Barking should be combined into one borough, which might also include the estate part of what is at present Ilford, the result should in time be unified local ownership, such as was envisaged originally by the L.C.C.

other, the better the chance of people getting to know their fellow residents.

This last point was recognized by the L.C.C.'s team which worked on the plans for the new town at Hook. They intended to build at average densities higher than those in Dagenham or the post-1945 new towns[1]—without, incidentally, more than a third of the dwellings being 'off the ground'—and they argued:

> 'The pattern of social relationships, neither simple, static nor closely predictable, may indeed be influenced by density.' They went on to say that their proposals would increase '. . . the possibility and frequency of accidental or intentional social encounters outside the home, through the concentration of pedestrian movement and local social buildings. Higher density does not force sociability on anyone, but does increase the choice of available shops, schools, pubs and acquaintances, near at hand.'[2]

I do not think there can be any doubt about this; if the planner is concerned about promoting social relationships between residents, he can use these three methods—'framing', arrangement of dwellings, and higher density. What can reasonably be argued is that most people are not concerned about 'sociability' of this kind, or that, even if they are, they care more about other things—larger gardens, a more open aspect—which are incompatible with high density. Let me look at these in turn. First, is 'sociability' important? It may not be for some people, but it obviously matters to many of those at Dagenham. The fact is that the people in the 'neighbourly' streets seem in the main to welcome the kind of social relations that have developed; they both enjoy their life and benefit from the mutual aid it involves. Similarly, some at least of those in other kinds

---

[1] Densities in new towns vary; though the *average* density of a new town, because of the flats provided, is often higher than Dagenham's 12 houses to the acre, many housing areas are at lower densities.

[2] *The Planning of a New Town*, p. 41; the relevance of density to social contact is illustrated diagrammatically by Figs. 33a, 33b and 33c on p. 41 in that report.

of street miss the 'East End spirit'. So for many working-class people, if not for others, 'planning for sociability', as one might call it, does serve a useful purpose.

Now to the other argument—that, even though people may value neighbourliness, most of them value more highly other things which cannot be provided at high densities. On gardens, my impression is that this is not so at Dagenham—that many people would be prepared to sacrifice some garden space in return for more privacy. The issue of privacy is, indeed, central to this argument about density. It seems clear that many who want to live at lower density than they do at present do so because they see this as the means to greater privacy. This concern with privacy was evident at Dagenham. I have already referred to the strains that can develop when people share front porches with their next-door neighbours. There were other examples, too. 'I like the house,' said Mrs. Ralph, 'but there's no privacy in the garden. You feel you're in a wilderness.' Mr. Gibson said, 'With these little fences they've got here, you can't do anything in the garden. It's not really private enough.' 'When the woman next door is chastising her children,' said Mr. Rank, 'or the man is mending his boots, you can hear the whole thing. It makes it more difficult to keep on good terms with them.'[1]

This is not as much of a contradiction as it seems to what has been suggested earlier—that most people at Dagenham either have neighbourly relationships with others, or would appreciate them. 'Privacy' means a number of things—but mainly reasonable protection from the sound of other people, and a parallel freedom to make a noise oneself; not being 'overlooked', and avoiding the embarrassment of 'overlooking' others. The fact is, I am certain, that most people want *both* privacy inside their own home and garden *and* the opportunity to get to know—and, to a greater or

---

[1] The same point was noted by Mass Observation 20 years ago, as these two quotations illustrate—'The fences in the gardens should be higher, not overlooking like this. A lot of people want more privacy.' 'The back garden fence should be higher, to make it more private.' Op. cit., p. 172.

lesser extent, mix with—others in the vicinity if they want to. And the higher the density, or the more compact the layout, the more essential privacy is in and around the dwelling (including in the garden).[1]

The implication of this is not, of course, that new communities should be formed exclusively of cul-de-sacs and the like, nor that their overall densities should necessarily be higher than in the present new towns. What one would hope for is a wide range of choice in homes being offered, which would include some layouts designed to work in the way the 'banjos' do.

Dagenham can also offer a suggestion, I believe, about the siting of amenities like shops and public houses. Small, really local pubs and corner shops have found no place in most post-war plans. Since town planning has been based upon the 'zoning' of different land-uses—an approach which has, fortunately, begun to be challenged recently among planners themselves—the shops and pubs in new communities have automatically formed part of tidy groups, at 'local centres' or 'town centres', not dispersed throughout the housing. But, as suggested in Chapter VII, corner shops and pubs can perform useful functions as social centres for the immediate vicinity, helping to create and maintain acquaintanceships between local people.[2] Even now, at Dagenham itself, there seems no reason why some appropriately sited corner houses might not be converted into local general shops with living accommodation. At least, this might be tried out on an experimental basis.

*   *   *   *   *

Continuity and change—these have been the recurrent

---

[1] This was the conclusion of the L.C.C.'s new town team. 'Densities must not be raised . . . to the point where privacy within the home is curtailed. The densities we propose can be achieved, without loss of privacy . . .' *The Planning of a New Town*, p. 41. Kuper came to a similar conclusion in his Coventry study—that where the layout provided 'many opportunities for contact between residents, relatively high standards of privacy in and around the immediate vicinity of the house are necessary'. Kuper, L., op. cit., p. 168.

[2] This, again, is something which was recommended, at least for 'corner shops', by the L.C.C.'s new town team. See *The Planning of a New Town*, p. 40.

themes of this survey. The migration from the East End to Dagenham started 40 years ago and is still in process. It created, and still creates, an upheaval in the lives of those who move. And many of the second generation have moved in their turn—some voluntarily, some more reluctantly. In each generation and in all classes some people willingly uproot themselves from their native district—in search of a better house, the 'country', 'fresh air', and, for some, a 'superior district'. But in each generation, too, many want to stay. As this survey has shown, many of the migrants to Dagenham, and their children, have settled and built in the new district a life which, in its social organization, is very like the old.

The various suggestions put forward in the preceding pages start from the fact of this similarity; their purpose is to enable people to re-create the 'traditional' patterns of life, if they wish to. For it is the resilience of these familiar forms of solidarity amongst the people of Dagenham which is, above all, so impressive.

APPENDIX 1

METHODS OF RESEARCH

As explained in the Introduction, three main samples of people were interviewed in this survey. These are discussed in turn.

The general sample

This is called a 'general' sample because it reflects the adult population of the estate as a whole, rather than any special group within it. With the help of the L.C.C.'s officers at Dagenham, we picked out from the Electoral Registers for the three local constituencies of Dagenham, Ilford and Barking the parts which applied to the estate. The registers used were those published in February 1958, from information collected in October 1957, and the relevant portions contained 66,393 names—39,390 in Dagenham, 20,269 in Barking and 6,734 in Ilford. From these we drew out 1,090 names and addresses. The response is shown in Table 10.

TABLE 10

RESPONSE IN GENERAL SURVEY

Names drawn	1,090
Not contacted (death, removal, etc.)	97
Number contacted	993
Refusals	116
Number interviewed	877

Expressed as a proportion of the initial sample, those who could not be contacted amounted to 9%; of those who were contacted, 12% refused an interview. These proportions are not unusual with a survey of this kind. Some basic facts about the composition of the sample interviewed are given in Tables 11 and 12.

127

TABLE 11

GENERAL SAMPLE, SEX AND MARITAL STATUS

	Men	*Women*	*Men and Women*
Married	82%	75%	78%
Widowed or Divorced* ..	3%	15%	9%
Single	15%	10%	13%
Total %	100%	100%	100%
Number	442	435	877

* One man and four women were divorced—less than 1% of the sample.

TABLE 12

GENERAL SAMPLE, SEX AND AGE

	Men	*Women*	*Men and Women*
20–29	15%	12%	14%
30–39	20%	19%	20%
40–49	21%	19%	20%
50–59	24%	25%	24%
60–69	16%	18%	17%
70 and over	4%	7%	5%
Total %	100%	100%	100%
Number	442	435	877

The interviews with the people in this sample were carried out by 15 interviewers working under our direction from an office in the Dagenham Borough Council's Central Library premises at Valence House. The interviews were formal and standardized, the questions straightforward and factual; with most there was a limited range of alternative answers. Questions were put, for example, on people's age, job, length of residence both on the estate and in their present house, and on the whereabouts

and last contacts with parents, parents-in-law, married children
and so on. The interview schedule used was closely akin to that
used in the general survey in Woodford, and the interested reader
is referred to *Family and Class in a London Suburb*, where the interview schedule is reproduced, together with a copy of the in-
structions issued to interviewers.[1]

The marriage sample

The general sample included 143 married subjects who were
living at home with their husband or wife and had two or more
children under 15. Some of these were selected for further interviewing, people at this stage in life being chosen because comparable groups had been interviewed in Bethnal Green and on the
post-1945 estate of Greenleigh. The method used at Dagenham
for drawing this 'sub-sample' from the general sample was as
follows: out of the 143 eligible subjects, names and addresses
were picked at randon until enough had been drawn to produce
a final sample of 50. In fact, 54 had to be selected, because three
people refused a further interview and one had moved away.

Fuller interviews were carried out with both husband and wife,
irrespective of which of them had been the subject in the general
survey. It would, of course, have been best if husband and wife
could have been interviewed independently, so as to have avoided
the danger of one influencing the replies of the other, but in practice it is never easy to arrange this. Of the 50 couples, 32 were seen
together, nine entirely separately, and the remaining nine partly
together, partly separately (e.g. the wife might be interviewed
alone, and then the husband interviewed later in her presence).

The interviews varied in length from about 40 minutes to over
two hours, and some people who were particularly co-operative,
or whose help was needed to elucidate a point, were called on
three or four times altogether. These interviews, carried out by
Ralph Samuel and myself, were relatively 'open' and 'unstruc-
tured', compared with those in the general survey. We had a
schedule of questions, which provided some kind of framework
for the interview, but within this we felt ourselves free to follow
up any 'leads' suggested by our informants. Questions were put
on the following main topics:

[1] *Family and Class in a London Suburb*, Appendix 2, pp. 139–58.

How people came to be living where they did.

People's opinions of, and work in, their house and garden.

Attitudes to moving.

'Friendliness.'

Visits from, and to, friends or neighbours.

Whereabouts of, and relationships with, both husband's and wife's parents, brothers and sisters and other relatives.

Attitudes to children's education.

Wife working—attitudes to, and how the family manages if she does.

Politics and social class (husbands only).

After each interview we wrote up, from our notes, a full interview report, including verbatim remarks where possible.

Some details about the marriage sample are given in Tables 13 to 16. As will be seen from Table 13, a majority of both husbands and wives were in their thirties, the others being mainly older rather than younger (none were over 49). More than half were married before 1946, as Table 14 shows; and with 23 couples the husband or wife or both had lived on the Dagenham estate before marriage, whereas 27 couples had moved to the estate after they married. It will be remembered that all those in the sample had at least two children. As Table 15 shows, half had two children only, and of the rest, roughly half had three, and half four or more. The ages of the youngest children are shown in Table 16.

In occupation, the husbands were much like men in the general sample, except that more were skilled and less unskilled. Only four had white-collar jobs, 33 were skilled manual workers, 11 semi-skilled and two unskilled.

TABLE 13
MARRIAGE SAMPLE, AGES OF HUSBANDS AND WIVES

	Husbands	*Wives*
Under 30	1	6
30–39	30	30
40–49	19	14
Total	50	50

TABLE 14

MARRIAGE SAMPLE, DATE OF MARRIAGE

Before 1940	16
1940–1945	13
1946–1949	16
1950 or later	5
Total	50

TABLE 15

MARRIAGE SAMPLE, NUMBER OF CHILDREN

Two children	25
Three children	13
Four or more	12
Total	50
Couples having children of 15 or over	16

TABLE 16

AGE OF YOUNGEST CHILD IN FAMILY

Under 5	16
6–9	23
10–15	11
Total	50

The tenants' sample

This was a further sub-sample selected from the general sample for further interviewing. In this instance, we wanted to talk to people—tenants or the wives of tenants—who had arrived on the estate in 1930 or earlier. There were 150 such people, and again names and addresses were picked at random until we had a final sample of 20; 22 had to be selected, because two refused to be interviewed further.

As with the marriage sample, the interviews, which were done by Phyllis Willmott and myself, were both relatively informal and relatively long—lasting between one and two hours. The following were the main topics:

First impressions of the estate, comparison with former district, and experiences in early years.

Changes in estate since beginning.

Attitude to, and work in, house and garden.

'Friendliness.'

Visits to, or from, friends or neighbours.

Questions on children—where living, how they came to live there, their attitude to the estate, etc. Also how often children, grandchildren and children-in-law seen, and occupations of children and children-in-law.

Again, a full report was written up after each interview.

The ages of the men and women in this sample are shown in Table 17.

TABLE 17

TENANTS' SAMPLE, SEX AND AGE

	Men	*Women*	*Men and Women*
50–59	—	8	8
60–69	5	4	9
70 and over	2	1	3
Total	7	13	20

As will be seen, most people were in their fifties or sixties, and women outnumbered men. All of the men were married, and ten of the women—the remaining three being widows. All had at least one child, and they had between them 68 children altogether, of whom 59 were married. Seventeen of this 59 lived on the estate, the rest elsewhere. Ten of the 20 people had no married child living on the estate—a similar proportion to that among people (with married children) in the general sample as a whole.

The problem of interpretation

A problem with any sample inquiry is how far the information collected from the sample applies to the wider population from which the sample was drawn. A method sometimes used to deal with this question is to carry out 'tests of statistical significance' on the material presented. The purpose of such tests is to determine, within specified limits of probability, whether apparent differences in the sample are likely to reflect differences in the population under study, or to be 'due to chance'—that is, to result from some bias in the sample. This use of 'tests of significance' has, however, been increasingly attacked in recent years, particularly by some American sociologists.[1] Their main criticism has been that these tests—the X^2 test, the t test, and so on—cannot properly be applied to data from social surveys, and that to use them and reproduce the results gives a bogus air of 'scientific' authority to one's findings. I find this argument convincing, and therefore do not reproduce a series of test results in this book.

I have, in deciding whether or not to include a particular result from the survey, done two things. The first was to carry out a series of further tables to try to see if apparent differences were explained by other, incidental, differences in the various groups under examination. Many scores of these further tabulations were carried out. I have also, on each particular issue, examined any relevant information from the survey—more 'impressionistic' material from the fuller interviews, as well as any statistical data available—in deciding what to say. Hence, since the information was not always as full as I would have liked, some of my 'conclusions' are less firm, are more tentative, than others. This book, therefore, is nothing like a final and authoritative work on Dagenham's patterns of behaviour. It is rather what seems to me, on the diverse and often inadequate information available, the most likely, the most plausible, description and explanation of what is going on there.

[1] See, e.g., Selvin, H. C., 'A Critique of Tests of Significance in Survey Research'.

APPENDIX 2

ADDITIONAL TABLES

In the course of the book, the reader is referred to a number of additional tables. They are set out here, under these headings: (1) a single table dealing with arrival on the estate, according to people's ages; (2) tables on visits from friends or neighbours; (3) a table on social class and social contacts; (4) tables on the social composition of different types of road on the estate; (5) tables on attendance at clubs, churches and public houses.

(1) *Age and arrival on estate* (see p. 21 and p. 41).

TABLE 18

ARRIVAL ON ESTATE, ACCORDING TO AGE OF INFORMANT

(General sample)

	21–29	30–39	40–49	50–59	60 and over	All ages
Born on the estate	25%	5%	2%	—	—	5%
Went to estate up to and including 1930 ..	4%	27%	17%	24%	47%	25%
Went to estate 1931–1939 ..	37%	20%	37%	55%	36%	38%
Went to estate 1940–1945 ..	12%	6%	20%	13%	10%	12%
Went to estate 1946 or later ..	22%	42%	24%	8%	7%	20%
Total % ..	100%	100%	100%	100%	100%	100%
Number ..	121	172	172	214	196	875

(2) *Visits from friends and neighbours* (see Chapters VI and VII)

TABLE 19

FRIENDS VISITING, ACCORDING TO SOCIAL CLASS
DAGENHAM AND WOODFORD COMPARED

(General samples)

	Dagenham		Woodford	
	White Collar*	Working Class	White Collar*	Working Class
% having visits from one or more friends or neighbours in previous 24 hours ..	43%	28%	42%	34%
Total number ..	94	696	580	355

* In Woodford, as in Dagenham, the term 'white collar' is applied to informants who had, or whose husbands had, non-manual occupations.

TABLE 20

FRIENDS VISITING, ACCORDING TO DATE
OF ARRIVAL ON ESTATE

(General sample)

	Born on estate	Arrived up to and including 1930	Arrived 1931–1939	Arrived 1940–1945	Arrived 1956 or later
% having visits from one or more friends or neighbours in previous 24 hours ..	29%	32%	27%	26%	34%
Total number	41	225	328	105	174

Additional Tables

TABLE 21

FRIENDS VISITING, ACCORDING TO DATE
OF MOVING INTO PRESENT HOUSE
(General sample)

	Up to and including 1939	1940–1945	1946–1955	1956 or later
% having visits from one or more friends or neighbours in previous 24 hours	28%	28%	33%	36%
Total number ..	356	128	292	70

3. *Social class and social contacts at Dagenham* (see p. 72)

TABLE 22

SOCIAL CLASS AND SOCIAL CONTACTS
(General sample)

		Working Class		
	White Collar	Skilled	Semi-skilled	Unskilled
% having visits from one or more friends or neighbours in previous 24 hours	43%	30%	27%	25%
% attending club or other social organization within previous month ..	16%	13%	7%	9%
% attending church within previous month ..	15%	8%	7%	5%
% visiting public house within previous month ..	22%	21%	21%	22%
Total number	94	358	194	144

Additional Tables

4. *Social composition of different types of road* (see Chapter VII)

The reader is referred to the layout diagram on p. xiv, for illustrations of the different types of road. The seven cul-de-sacs ('banjos') can clearly be seen. The roads labelled 'Wood Lane' and 'Heathway' are regarded as 'main roads', and all other roads shown would be described as 'side roads'.

TABLE 23

LENGTH OF TIME IN PRESENT HOUSE,
ACCORDING TO TYPE OF ROAD
(General Sample)

	Main road	*Side road*	*Cul-de-sac*
Up to and including 1939	40%	44%	37%
1940–1945	17%	14%	19%
1946–1955	34%	34%	38%
1956 or later	9%	8%	6%
Total %	100%	100%	100%
Number	166	599	82

TABLE 24

OCCUPATIONAL CLASS, ACCORDING TO TYPE OF ROAD
(General sample)

	Main road	*Side road*	*Cul-de-sac*
Professional and managerial	5%	3%	5%
Clerical and shop workers	7%	9%	4%
Skilled manual ..	50%	46%	43%
Semi-skilled manual	23%	23%	36%
Unskilled manual ..	15%	19%	12%
Total %	100%	100%	100%
Number ..	163	550	76

TABLE 25
AGE OF INFORMANT, ACCORDING TO
TYPE OF ROAD
(General sample)

	Main road	*Side road*	*Cul-de-sac*
20–29	18%	13%	12%
30–39	17%	19%	25%
40–49	17%	20%	24%
50–59	28%	24%	23%
60–69	17%	18%	10%
70 or over	3%	6%	6%
Total %	100%	100%	100%
Number	175	619	83

(5) *Clubs, churches and public houses* (see Chapter VIII)

Tables 26 and 27 deal with the question of whether people who do not have visits from friends or relatives more often belong to clubs. The conclusion is that there is no evidence this kind of 'compensation' is taking place to any marked extent. On the contrary, it looks as if those visited by friends belong to clubs more often.

TABLE 26
CLUB MEMBERSHIP AND ATTENDANCE,
ACCORDING TO WHETHER VISITED BY FRIEND OR NEIGHBOUR
(General sample)

	Visited by one or more friends or neighbours in previous 24 hours	*Not visited*
Attended at least one club or social organization within previous month	17%	10%
Not attended within previous month, but member of at least one club or social organization ..	8%	4%
Not member of any club or social organization	75%	86%
Total %	100%	100%
Number	263	611

TABLE 27
CLUB MEMBERSHIP AND ATTENDANCE,
ACCORDING TO WHETHER VISITED BY RELATIVE
(General sample)

	Visited by one or more relatives in previous 24 hours	*Not visited*
Attended at least one club or social organization within previous month	10%	13%
Not attended within previous month, but member of at least one club or social organization ..	5%	5%
Not member of any club or social organization	85%	82%
Total %	100%	100%
Number	209	664

In connexion with Tables 28 to 30, the reader should note that the term 'white collar', in Woodford as in Dagenham, applies to people who have, or women married to men who have, non-manual jobs.

TABLE 28
CLUB MEMBERSHIP AND ATTENDANCE IN DAGENHAM
AND WOODFORD, ACCORDING TO SOCIAL CLASS
(General sample)

	Dagenham		*Woodford*	
	White Collar	*Working Class*	*White Collar*	*Working Class*
Attended at least one club or social organization within previous month ..	16%	11%	35%	18%
Not attended within previous month, but member of at least one club or social organization ..	7%	5%	17%	16%
Not member of any club or social organization ..	77%	84%	48%	66%
Total %	100%	100%	100%	100%
Number	94	696	580	355

TABLE 29
CHURCH ATTENDANCE IN DAGENHAM AND WOODFORD ACCORDING TO SOCIAL CLASS
(General samples)

	Dagenham		Woodford	
	White Collar	Working Class	White Collar	Working Class
Attended church within previous month ..	15%	7%	34%	17%
Not attended within previous month but go to church	12%	10%	26%	26%
Never go to church ..	73%	83%	40%	57%
Total %	100%	100%	100%	100%
Number	94	696	580	355

TABLE 30
VISITS TO PUBLIC HOUSES IN DAGENHAM AND WOODFORD, ACCORDING TO SOCIAL CLASS
(General samples)

	Dagenham		Woodford	
	White Collar	Working Class	White Collar	Working Class
Visited public house within previous month	22%	22%	47%	35%
Not visited within previous month, but sometimes go to public house	7%	15%	21%	22%
Never go to pub ..	71%	63%	32%	43%
Total %	100%	100%	100%	100%
Number	94	696	580	355

APPENDIX 3

LONDON COUNTY COUNCIL'S HOUSE-ROOM STANDARDS

THE extent of overcrowding and under-occupation on the Dagenham estate is discussed in Chapter IV. An obvious difficulty is deciding whether a family has 'too much' or 'too little' room in its present dwelling, is what standard one should use. I have followed the London County Council's own standards, which are set out below; I am grateful to the L.C.C. for permission to reproduce them. I should explain that the L.C.C.'s standards of overcrowding are more generous than the statutory standards (as laid down in the Housing Act, 1957, Section 77 and Sixth Schedule). In other words, the L.C.C. would regard as 'overcrowded' and therefore needing more room, many families which would, in the statutory standards, not be considered overcrowded. The following statement was issued by the L.C.C.'s Housing Department in 1960:

RATIONING OF ACCOMMODATION

In the allocation of accommodation at the Council's housing estates, the following general principles shall be observed:

(i) The accommodation allotted shall be sufficient to meet the reasonable needs of the families, taking into consideration the number of persons to be accommodated and the sex and ages of the children, provided that in no circumstances shall the number of persons to be accommodated exceed the scale laid down in the Fifth Schedule to the Housing Act, 1936.

(ii) One-room flats shall be let only to one person, two persons of the same sex, an adult with one child, or an aged married couple; and no person residing alone shall be accepted as a tenant except for such a flat.

(iii) Not more than two rooms shall be allotted to a married couple without children or to two persons of the same sex living together; provided that the Director of Housing may in special circumstances allot to an applicant larger accommodation than that prescribed on the understanding that preferential treatment shall not be given to the detriment of other applicants.

(iv) The grading of accommodation in excess of two rooms shall normally be as follows:—

3 rooms (2 bedrooms)—Couple with one child or two children of the same sex or two children of the opposite sex if either is less than 3 years of age

4 rooms (3 bedrooms)—Couple with two children of opposite sex over 6 and over 3 years of age respectively, or say up to four children

provided that—

(*a*) the offer of a tenancy of a four-room or five-room dwelling, particularly when the children of the family are likely to need more accommodation in a reasonable period of time (instead of a three-room or four-room dwelling, respectively), be authorized where the allocation would assist in implementing the Council's policy of allocation according to relative need;

(*b*) an existing tenant who has two or more rooms in excess of his requirements and who will not transfer otherwise, be allocated on transfer sufficient accommodation for his needs plus one spare room;

(*c*) the Director of Housing be authorized, in order to avoid delays in development of housing sites where the possession of premises involving the rehousing of the occupants is necessary, to offer at his discretion larger accommodation than that which the occupier would normally be offered.

APPENDIX 4

LIST OF REFERENCES

ABRAMS, M. and ROSE, R. *Must Labour Lose?* Harmondsworth, Penguin Books. 1960.

BAKKE, E. W. *The Unemployed Man*. London, Nisbet. 1933.

BENNEY, M., GRAY, A. P. and PEAR, R. H. *How People Vote*. London, Routledge & Kegan Paul. 1956.

BERGER, B. M. *Working-Class Suburb*. Berkeley and Los Angeles, University of California Press. 1960.

BOTT, E. *Family and Social Network*. London, Tavistock Publications. 1957.

BOTTOMORE, T. 'Social Stratification in Voluntary Organisations'. GLASS, D. V. (ed.) *Social Mobility in Britain*. London, Routledge & Kegan Paul. 1954.

BRENNAN, T. *Reshaping a City*. Glasgow, House of Grant. 1959.

CANNON, L. 'Mum'. *Dagenham Digest*. No. 50. January, 1961.

CAPLOW, T. and FOREMAN, R. 'Neighbourhood Interaction in a Homogeneous Community'. *American Sociological Review*. Vol. 15 No. 6. 1950.

CAUTER, T. and DOWNHAM, J. S. *The Communication of Ideas*. London, Chatto and Windus. 1954.

CHAMBERLIN, POWELL and BON, SHANKLAND, G. and JONES, D. G. 'The Living Suburb'. *Architecture and Building*. Vol. XXXIII. No. 9. September. 1958.

CULLINGWORTH, J. B. *Housing in Greater London*. London, London School of Economics and Political Science. 1961.

DONNISON, D. V., COCKBURN, C. and CORLETT, T. *Housing Since the Rent Act*. Occasional Papers on Social Administration. No. 3. Welwyn, Codicote Press. 1961.

DURANT, R. *Watling: A Survey of Social Life on a New Housing Estate*. London, P. S. King. 1939.

FESTINGER, L. 'Architecture and Group Membership'. *Journal of Social Issues*. Vol. 7, Nos. 1 & 2. 1951.

FESTINGER, L., SCHACHTER, S. and BACK, K. *Social Pressures in Informal Groups*. New York, Harper. 1950.

List of References

GANS, H. J. 'Planning and Social Life'. *Journal of the American Institute of Planners.* Vol. XXVII. No. 2. 1961.

GANS, H. J. 'The Balanced Community: Homogeneity or Heterogeneity in Residential Areas?' *Journal of the American Institute of Planners.* Vol. XXVII. No. 3. 1961.

GLASS, R. 'Social Aspects of Town Planning'. *Town and Country Planning Textbook.* (Association for Planning and Rural Reconstruction.) London, Architectural Press. 1950.

HOLE, V. 'Social Effects of Planned Rehousing'. *Town Planning Review.* Vol. 30. No. 2. July 1959.

HOLMES, A. R. *Investigation into Effects of Rehousing by the L.C.C.* M.Sc. Thesis. London University. 1947.

HUTCHINSON, B. *Willesden and the New Towns.* London, The Social Survey. Central Office of Information. 1947.

JACKSON, B. and MARSDEN, D. *Education and the Working Class.* London, Routledge & Kegan Paul. 1962.

JEFFERYS, M. *Mobility in the Labour Market.* London, Routledge & Kegan Paul. 1954.

JENNINGS, H. *Societies in the Making.* London, Routledge & Kegan Paul. 1962.

JEVONS, R. and MADGE, J. *Housing Estates.* Bristol, Arrowsmith. 1946.

KERR, M. *The People of Ship Street.* London, Routledge & Kegan Paul. 1958.

KUPER, L. 'Blueprint for Living Together'. KUPER, L. (ed.) *Living in Towns.* London, Cresset Press. 1953.

LIPSET, S. M. *Political Man.* London, Heinemann. 1960.

LLOYD, T. A. *Planning in Town and Country.* London, George Routledge & Sons. 1935.

LOCKWOOD, D. 'The "New Working Class" '. *European Journal of Sociology.* Vol. I. No. 2. 1960.

MARTIN, F. M., BROTHERSTON, J. H. F. and CHAVE, S. P. W. 'Incidence of Neurosis on a New Housing Estate'. *British Journal of Preventive and Social Medicine.* Vol. 11. No. 4. 1957.

MARTIN, F. M. 'Some Subjective Aspects of Social Stratification'. GLASS, D. V. (ed.) *Social Mobility in Britain.* London, Routledge & Kegan Paul. 1954.

MASS-OBSERVATION. *People's Homes.* London, John Murray. 1943.

MERTON, R. K. 'The Social Psychology of Housing'. DENNIS, W.

(ed.) *Current Trends in Social Psychology.* Pittsburgh, University of Pittsburgh Press. 1956.

MEYERSOHN, R. and JACKSON, R. 'Gardening in Suburbia'. DOBRINER, W. (Ed.) *The Suburban Community.* New York, Putnam. 1958.

MILNE, R. S. and MACKENZIE, H. C. *Marginal Seat 1955.* London, Hansard Society. 1958.

MITCHELL, G. D., LUPTON, T., HODGES, M. W. and SMITH, C. S. *Neighbourhood and Community.* Liverpool, Liverpool University Press. 1954.

MOGEY, J. M. *Family and Neighbourhood.* London, Oxford University Press. 1956.

MOSER, C. A. and SCOTT, W. *British Towns.* Edinburgh and London, Oliver and Boyd. 1961.

NICHOLSON, J. H. *New Communities in Britain.* London, National Council of Social Service. 1961.

O'LEARY, J. G. *Dagenham Place Names.* London, Borough of Dagenham. 1958.

O'LEARY, J. G. *The Book of Dagenham.* London, Borough of Dagenham. Second edition. 1949.

ORLANS, H. *Stevenage: A Sociological Study of a New Town.* London, Routledge & Kegan Paul. 1952.

OSBORN, F. J. *Green Belt Cities.* London, Faber and Faber. 1946.

P.E.P. 'Town and Country Planning'. *Planning.* Vol. 1. No. 2. 1933.

RICHARDSON, M. *Post-War Population and Housing Trends in Metropolitan Essex.* Thesis for Diploma in Town Planning. London, Regent Street Polytechnic. 1962.

ROBSON, W. A. *The Government and Misgovernment of London.* London, Allen & Unwin. 1939.

SELVIN, H. C. 'A Critique of Tests of Significance in Survey Research'. *American Sociological Review.* Vol. 22. No. 5. 1957.

SILKIN, L. 'Housing Layout in Theory and Practice'. *Journal of the Royal Institute of British Architects.* Vol. 55. No. 10. 1948.

SINCLAIR, R. *Metropolitan Man.* London, Allen & Unwin. 1937.

STACEY, M. *Tradition and Change.* London, Oxford University Press. 1960.

TÖNNIES, F. *Community and Association.* London, Routledge & Kegan Paul. 1955.

TOWNSEND, P. *The Family Life of Old People.* London, Routledge & Kegan Paul. 1957.

List of References

VEREKER, C., MAYS, J. B. *et al. Urban Redevelopment and Social Change.* Liverpool, Liverpool University Press. 1961.

WHITE, L. E. *Community or Chaos: Housing Estates and their Social Problems.* London, National Council of Social Service. 1950.

WHITE, L. E. *New Towns.* London, National Council of Social Service. 1951.

WHYTE, W. H. *The Organisation Man.* London, Cape. 1957.

WILLIAMS, N. *Population Problems of New Estates.* Liverpool, Liverpool University Press. 1939.

WILLMOTT, P. and BARBOUR, P. 'Housing of Old People in a Rural Parish'. *Social Service Quarterly.* Vol. XXXI. No. 4. 1958.

WILLMOTT, P. and YOUNG, M. *Family and Class in a London Suburb.* London, Routledge & Kegan Paul. 1960.

WILLMOTT, P. 'Housing Density and Town Design in a New Town'. *Town Planning Review.* Vol. 33. No. 2. 1962.

YOUNG, M. and WILLMOTT, P. *Family and Kinship in East London.* London, Routledge & Kegan Paul. 1957.

YOUNG, T. *Becontree and Dagenham.* London, Becontree Social Survey Committee. 1934.

Annual Abstract of Statistics. No. 98. London, H.M.S.O. 1961.

Census 1951. England and Wales. County Report: London. London, H.M.S.O. 1953.

Census 1951. England and Wales. Occupation Tables. London, H.M.S.O. 1956.

Classification of Occupations, 1950. London, H.M.S.O. 1956.

L.C.C. *Administrative County of London Development Plan, First Review 1960. County Planning Report.* London, London County Council. 1960.

L.C.C. Council Minutes. *Housing Committee Report* 22 June, 1926.

L.C.C. *London Housing Statistics, 1958–59.* London, London County Council. 1959.

L.C.C. *Report* by the Architect and Director of Housing to the Housing (Building and Development) Sub-Committee, 25 February, 1920.

L.C.C. *The Planning of a New Town.* London, London County Council. 1961.

London Government: Government Proposals for Re-organisation. London, H.M.S.O. 1961.

Royal Commission on Local Government in Greater London. *Minutes of Evidence.* London, H.M.S.O. 1959.

INDEX

Abrams, M., 97n, 105n, 106n
Accommodation; overcrowding and under-occupation of, 39–40, 120
    rationing of by L.C.C., 141–2
Age; and sociability, 71, 82
    by date of arrival at Dagenham, 134
    children of marriage sample, 131
    difficulties of moving in old, 40
    general sample, 128
    marriage sample, 130
    of informant, according to type of road, 138
    of youngest child, marriage sample, 131
    tenants' sample, 132
Age-structure; at Dagenham compared with Bethnal Green and England and Wales, 22–24
    in new communities, 119
Amenities; in early days, 9–11
    lack of, today, 110
    siting of, 125
Architecture of Estate, 1–3, 52, 110
Arrival at Dagenham; according to age, 134
    and friends visiting, 135
    date of, 22
    early days, 6–11

Back, K., 81n
Bakke, E. W., 65n
Baldwin, S., 11
Banbury, 84n
'Banjos', see Cul-de-sacs
Barbour, P., 40n
Barking, x, 2, 17, 19, 38, 41, 43–44, 122n, 128
Barton Hill, vii, 88n
Basildon, 119

Becontree, x See also Dagenham
Benney, M., 104n
Berger, B. M., 111n
Bethnal Green; family life in, 30, 33
    friends and friendliness in, 19, 64–65
    length of residence in, 22
    occupational class of men in, 14
    old people's membership of clubs in, 86
    physical layout of, 83, 88–89
    politics of, 104
    proximity of married children in, 35, 45
    public houses in, 87–88
    shops in, 88
    size of dwellings in, 39
    size of population of, 24–25
    social patterns of, vii, 50, 67, 83, 86–89, 111
    wives working in, 60n
Boston Manor, 120
Bott, E., 103n
Bottomore, T., 84n
Brennan, T., viin
Bristol; conversion of council houses in, 120n
    references to, vii, 12n, 32n, 56n, 88n, 120n, 121
Brothers and sisters at Dagenham, 26
Brotherston, J. H. F., viiin

Cannon, L., 50n
Canvey Island, 38
Caplow, T., 81n
Cars; at Dagenham, 96–97
    Dagenham and Woodford compared, 89
Cauter, T., 84n
Census, 1951, 39

147

Index

148

The International Library of

Sociology

and Social Reconstruction

Edited by **W. J. H. SPROTT**
Founded by **KARL MANNHEIM**

ROUTLEDGE & KEGAN PAUL

BROADWAY HOUSE, CARTER LANE, LONDON, E.C.4

CONTENTS

PRINTED IN GREAT BRITAIN BY HEADLEY BROTHERS LTD
109 KINGSWAY LONDON W C 2 AND ASHFORD KENT

GENERAL SOCIOLOGY

Gibson, Quentin. The Logic of Social Enquiry. *240 pp. 1960. 24s.*

Goldschmidt, Professor Walter. Understanding Human Society. *272 pp. 1959. 21s.*

Johnson, Harry M. Sociology: a Systematic Introduction. *Foreword by Robert K. Merton. 710 pp. 1961. (2nd Impression 1962.) 42s.*

Mannheim, Karl. Essays on Sociology and Social Psychology. *Edited by Paul Keckskemeti. With Editorial Note by Adolph Lowe. 344 pp. 1953. 30s.*
Systematic Sociology: An Introduction to the Study of Society. *Edited by J. S. Erös and Professor W. A. C. Stewart. 220 pp. 1957. (2nd Impression 1959.) 24s.*

Martindale, Don. The Nature and Types of Sociological Theory. *292 pp. 1961. 35s.*

Maus, Heinz. A Short History of Sociology. *234 pp. 1962. 28s.*

Myrdal, Gunnar. Value in Social Theory: A Collection of Essays on Methodology. *Edited by Paul Streeten. 332 pp. 1958. (2nd Impression 1962.) 32s.*

Ogburn, William F., and **Nimkoff, Meyer F.** A Handbook of Sociology. *Preface by Karl Mannheim. 612 pp. 46 figures. 38 tables. 4th edition (revised) 1960. 35s.*

Parsons, Talcott and **Smelser, Neil J.** Economy and Society: A Study in the Integration of Economic and Social Theory. *362 pp. 1956. (2nd Impression 1957.) 35s.*

Rex, John. Key Problems of Sociological Theory. *220 pp. 1961. 25s.*

FOREIGN CLASSICS OF SOCIOLOGY

Durkheim, Emile. Suicide. A Study in Sociology. *Edited and with an Introduction by George Simpson. 404 pp. 1952. 30s.*
Socialism and Saint-Simon. *Edited with an Introduction by Alvin W. Gouldner. Translated by Charlotte Sattler from the edition originally edited with an Introduction by Marcel Mauss. 286 pp. 1959. 28s.*
Professional Ethics and Civic Morals. *Translated by Cornelia Brookfield. 288 pp. 1957. 30s.*

Gerth, H. H., and **Wright Mills, C.** From Max Weber: Essays in Sociology. *502 pp. 1948. (4th Impression 1961.) 32s.*

Tönnies, Ferdinand. Community and Association. (*Gemeinschaft und Gesellschaft.) Translated and Supplemented by Charles P. Loomis. Foreword by Pitirim A. Sorokin. 334 pp. 1955. 25s.*

SOCIAL STRUCTURE

Andrzejewski, Stanislaw. Military Organization and Society. *With a Foreword by Professor A. R. Radcliffe-Brown. 226 pp. 1 folder. 1954. 21s.*

Cole, G. D. H. Studies in Class Structure. *220 pp. 1955. (2nd Impression 1961.) 21s.*

Coontz, Sydney H. Population Theories and the Economic Interpretation. *202 pp. 1957. (2nd Impression 1961.) 25s.*

Coser, Lewis. The Functions of Social Conflict. *204 pp. 1956. 18s.*

Eisenstadt, S. N. From Generation to Generation: Age Groups and Social Structure. *374 pp. 1956. 42s.*

Kelsall, R. K. Higher Civil Servants in Britain: From 1870 to the Present Day. *268 pp. 31 tables. 1955. 25s.*

Marsh, David C. The Changing Social Structure of England and Wales, 1871-1951. *296 pp. 63 tables. 1958. 28s.*

SOCIOLOGY AND POLITICS

Barbu, Zevedei. Democracy and Dictatorship: Their Psychology and Patterns of Life. *300 pp. 1956. 28s.*

Benney, Mark, Gray, A. P., and **Pear, R. H.** How People Vote: a Study of Electoral Behaviour in Greenwich. *Foreword by Professor W. A. Robson. 256 pp. 70 tables. 1956. 25s.*

Bramstedt, Dr. E. K. Dictatorship and Political Police: The Technique of Control by Fear. *286 pp. 1945. 20s.*

Crick, Bernard. The American Science of Politics: Its Origins and Conditions. *284 pp. 1959. 28s.*

Hertz, Frederick. Nationality in History and Politics: A Psychology and Sociology of National Sentiment and Nationalism. *440 pp. 1944. (4th Impression 1957.) 32s.*

Kornhauser, William. The Politics of Mass Society. *272 pp. 20 tables. 1960. 25s.*

Laidler, Harry W. Social-Economic Movements: An Historical and Comparative Survey of Socialism, Communism, Co-operation, Utopianism; and other Systems of Reform and Reconstruction. *864 pp. 16 plates. 1 figure. 1949. (3rd Impression 1960.) 50s.*

Mannheim, Karl. Freedom, Power and Democratic Planning. *Edited by Hans Gerth and Ernest K. Bramstedt. 424 pp. 1951. 35s.*

Myrdal, Gunnar. The Political Element in the Development of Economic Theory. *Translated from the German by Paul Streeten. 282 pp. 1953. (3rd Impression 1961.) 25s.*

Polanyi, Michael, F.R.S. The Logic of Liberty: Reflections and Rejoinders. *228 pp. 1951. 18s.*

Verney, Douglas V. The Analysis of Political Systems. *264 pp. 1959. (2nd Impression 1961.) 28s.*

FOREIGN AFFAIRS: THEIR SOCIAL, POLITICAL AND ECONOMIC FOUNDATIONS

Bonné, Alfred. The Economic Development of the Middle East: An Outline of Planned Reconstruction after the War. *192 pp. 58 tables. 1945. (3rd Impression 1953.) 16s.*
State and Economics in the Middle East: A Society in Transition. *482 pp. 2nd (revised) edition 1955. (2nd Impression 1960.) 40s.*
Studies in Economic Development: with special reference to Conditions in the Under-developed Areas of Western Asia and India. *322 pp. 84 tables. (2nd edition 1960.) 32s.*

Douglas, Dorothy W. Transitional Economic Systems. The Polish-Czech Example. *384 pp. 1953. 25s.*

Hughes, Everett C. French Canada in Transition. *252 pp. 49 tables. 16 figures. 4 maps. 1946. 16s.*

Mayer, J. P. Political Thought in France from the Revolution to the Fifth Republic. *164 pp. 3rd edition (revised) 1961. 16s.*

Schenk, H. G. The Aftermath of the Napoleonic Wars: The Concert of Europe—an Experiment. *250 pp. 17 plates. 1947. 18s.*

Schlesinger, Rudolf. Central European Democracy and its Background: Economic and Political Group Organization. *432 pp. 1953. 30s.*

Thomson, David, Meyer, E., and Briggs, A. Patterns of Peacemaking. *408 pp. 1945. 25s.*

Trouton, Ruth. Peasant Renaissance in Yugoslavia, 1900-1950: A Study of the Development of Yugoslav Peasant Society as affected by Education. *370 pp. 1 map. 1952. 28s.*

SOCIOLOGY OF LAW

Gurvitch, Dr. Georges. Sociology of Law. *With a Preface by Professor Roscoe Pound. 280 pp. 1947. (2nd Impression 1953.) 24s.*

Renner, Karl. The Institutions of Private Law and Their Social Functions. *Edited, with an Introduction and Notes by O. Kahn-Freund. Translated by Agnes Schwarzschild. 336 pp. 1949. 28s.*

CRIMINOLOGY

Cloward, Richard A., and Ohlin, Lloyd E. Delinquency and Opportunity: A Theory of Delinquent Gangs. *248 pp. 1961. 25s.*

Friedländer, Dr. Kate. The Psycho-Analytical Approach to Juvenile Delinquency: Theory, Case Studies, Treatment. *320 pp. 1947. (5th Impression 1961.) 25s.*

Glueck, Sheldon and Eleanor. Family Environment and Delinquency. *With the statistical assistance of Rose W. Kneznek. 340 pp. 1962. 35s.*

Grygier, Tadeusz. Oppression: a Study in Social and Criminal Psychology. *Foreword by Hermann Mannheim. 392 pp. 1954. 28s.*

Mannheim, Hermann. Group Problems in Crime and Punishment, and other Studies in Criminology and Criminal Law. *336 pp. 1955. 28s.*

Morris, Terence. The Criminal Area: A Study in Social Ecology. *Foreword by Hermann Mannheim. 232 pp. 25 tables. 4 maps. 1957. 25s.*

Spencer, John C. Crime and the Services. *Foreword by Hermann Mannheim. 336 pp. 1954. 28s.*

Trasler, Gordon. The Explanation of Criminality. *144 pp. 1962. 20s.*

SOCIAL PSYCHOLOGY

Barbu, Zevedei. Problems of Historical Psychology. *248 pp. 1960. 25s.*

Blackburn, Julian. Psychology and the Social Pattern. *184 pp. 1945. (6th Impression 1961.) 16s.*
The Framework of Human Behaviour. *182 pp. 1947. (2nd Impression 1953.) 15s.*

Fleming, C. M. Adolescence: Its Social Psychology: With an Introduction to recent findings from the fields of Anthropology, Physiology, Medicine, Psychometrics and Sociometry. *288 pp. (2nd edition 1962.) 18s.*
The Social Psychology of Education: An Introduction and Guide to Its Study. *136 pp. (2nd edition (revised) 1959.) 11s.*

Fleming, C. M. (Ed.). Studies in the Social Psychology of Adolescence. *Contributions by J. E. Richardson, J. F. Forrester, J. K. Shukla and P. J. Higginbotham. Foreword by the editor. 292 pp. 29 figures. 13 tables. 5 folder tables. 1951. 23s.*

Halmos, Paul. Solitude and Privacy: a Study of Social Isolation, its Causes and Therapy. *With a Foreword by Professor T. H. Marshall. 216 pp. 1952. 21s.*
Towards a Measure of Man: The Frontiers of Normal Adjustment. *276 pp. 1957. 28s.*

Hollitscher, Walter. Sigmund Freud: An Introduction. A Presentation of his Theory, and a Discussion of the Relationship between Psycho-Analysis and Sociology. *140 pp. 1947. (2nd Impression 1950.) 12s.*

Homans, George C. The Human Group. *Foreword by Bernard DeVoto. Introduction by Robert K. Merton. 526 pp. 1951. (3rd Impression 1959.) 28s.*
Social Behaviour: its Elementary Forms. *416 pp. 1961. 30s.*

Klein, Josephine. The Study of Groups. *226 pp. 31 figures. 5 tables. 1956. (3rd Impression 1962.) 21s.*

Linton, Ralph. The Cultural Background of Personality. *132 pp. 1947. (4th Impression 1958.) 16s.*
See also Yang, M.

Mayo, Elton. The Social Problems of an Industrial Civilization. With an appendix on the Political Problem. *180 pp. 1949. (4th Impression 1961.) 15s.*

Ridder, J. C. de. The Personality of the Urban African in South Africa. A Thematic Apperception Test Study. *196 pp. 12 plates. 1961. 25s.*

Rose, Arnold M. (Ed.). Mental Health and Mental Disorder: A Sociological Approach. *Chapters by 46 contributors. 654 pp. 1956. 40s.*
Human Behavior and Social Processes: an Interactionist Approach. *Contributions by Arnold M. Ross, Ralph H. Turner, Anselm Strauss, Everett C. Hughes, E. Franklin Frazier, Howard S. Becker, et al. 696 pp. 1962. 56s.*

Spinley, Dr. B. M. The Deprived and the Privileged: Personality Development in English Society. *232 pp. 1953. 20s.*

Wolfenstein, Martha. Disaster: A Psychological Essay. *264 pp. 1957. 23s.*

Young, Professor Kimball. Personality and Problems of Adjustment. *742 pp. 12 figures. 9 tables. 2nd edition (revised) 1952. (2nd Impression 1959.) 40s.*
Handbook of Social Psychology. *658 pp. 16 figures. 10 tables. 2nd edition (revised) 1957. (2nd Impression 1960.) 35s.*

SOCIOLOGY OF THE FAMILY

Banks, J. A. Prosperity and Parenthood: A Study of Family Planning among the Victorian Middle Classes. *262 pp. 1954. 24s.*

Chapman, Dennis. The Home and Social Status. *336 pp. 8 plates. 3 figures. 117 tables. 1955. 35s.*

Folsom, Joseph K. The Family and Democratic Society. *With chapters in collaboration with Marion Bassett. 782 pp. 1948. 35s.*

Klein, Viola. The Feminine Character: History of an Ideology. *With a Foreword by Karl Mannheim. 256 pp. 1946. 16s.*

Myrdal, Alva and **Klein, Viola.** Women's Two Roles: Home and Work. *238 pp. 27 tables. 1956. 25s.*

Parsons, Talcott and **Bales, Robert F.** Family: Socialization and Interaction Process. *In collaboration with James Olds, Morris Zelditch and Philip E. Slater. 456 pp. 50 figures and tables. 1956. 35s.*

THE SOCIAL SERVICES

Ashdown, Margaret and **Brown, S. Clement.** Social Service and Mental Health: An Essay on Psychiatric Social Workers. *280 pp. 1953. 21s.*

Hall, M. Penelope. The Social Services of Modern England. *416 pp. 5th edition (revised) 1960. 28s.*

Heywood, Jean S. Children in Care: the Development of the Service for the Deprived Child. *256 pp. 1959. 25s.*

Jones, Kathleen. Lunacy, Law and Conscience, 1744-1845: the Social History of the Care of the Insane. *268 pp. 1955. 25s.*
Mental Health and Social Policy, 1845-1959. *264 pp. 1960. 28s.*

Jones, Kathleen and **Sidebotham, Roy.** Mental Hospitals at Work. *220 pp. 1962. 30s.*

Kastell, Jean. Casework in Child Care. *Foreword by M. Brooke Willis. 320 pp. 1962.*

Rooff, Madeline. Voluntary Societies and Social Policy. *350 pp. 15 tables. 1957. 35s.*

Shenfield, B. E. Social Policies for Old Age: A Review of Social Provision for Old Age in Great Britain. *260 pp. 39 tables. 1957. 25s.*

Trasler, Gordon. In Place of Parents: A Study in Foster Care. *272 pp. 1960. 25s.*

Young, A. F., and **Ashton, E. T.** British Social Work in the Nineteenth Century. *288 pp. 1956. 25s.*

SOCIOLOGY OF EDUCATION

Banks, Olive. Parity and Prestige in English Secondary Education: a Study in Educational Sociology. *272 pp. 1955. 25s.*

Collier, K. G. The Social Purposes of Education: Personal and Social Values in Education. *268 pp. 1959. (2nd Impression 1962.) 21s.*

Connell, W. F. The Educational Thought and Influence of Matthew Arnold. *With an Introduction by Sir Fred Clarke. 332 pp. 1950. 23s.*

Cumming, Ian. Helvetius: His Life and Place in the History of Educational Thought. *With an Introduction by Nicholas Hans. 288 pp. Frontispiece. 1 folder. 1955. 25s.*

Dale, R. R. From School to University: A Study with special reference to University Entrance. *288 pp. 23 tables. 1954. 21s.*

Evans, K. M. Sociometry and Education. *158 pp. 1962. 18s.*

Gasset, José Ortega y. Mission of the University. *Translated with an Introduction by Howard Lee Nostrand. 104 pp. 1946. (2nd Impression 1952.) 12s. 6d.*

Hans, Nicholas. New Trends in Education in the Eighteenth Century. *278 pp. 19 tables. 1951. 25s.*
Comparative Education: A Study of Educational Factors and Traditions. *360 pp. 3rd (revised) edition 1958. (2nd Impression 1961.) 23s.*

Jacks, M. L. Total Education: A Plea for Synthesis. *184 pp. 1946. (4th Impression 1955.) 16s.*

Mannheim, Karl and **Stewart, W. A. C.** An Introduction to the Sociology of Education. *208 pp. 1962. 21s.*

Ottaway, A. K. C. Education and Society: An Introduction to the Sociology of Education. *With an Introduction by W. O. Lester Smith. 212 pp. 1953. (4th Impression 1960.) 18s.*

Peers, Robert. Adult Education: A Comparative Study. *398 pp. 2nd edition 1959. 35s.*

Samuel, R. H., and **Thomas, R. Hinton.** Education and Society in Modern Germany. *212 pp. 1949. 16s.*

Wittlin, Alma S. The Museum: Its History and its Tasks in Education. *328 pp. 24 plates. 18 figures. 1949. 28s.*

SOCIOLOGY OF CULTURE

Fromm, Erich. The Fear of Freedom. *286 pp. 1942. (8th Impression 1960.) 21s.* The Sane Society. *400 pp. 1956. (2nd Impression 1959.) 28s.*

Mannheim, Karl. Diagnosis of Our Time: Wartime Essays of a Sociologist. *208 pp. 1943. (7th Impression 1962.) 18s.* Essays on the Sociology of Culture. *Edited by Ernst Mannheim in cooperation with Paul Kecskemeti. Editorial Note by Adolph Lowe. 280 pp. 1956. (2nd Impression 1962.) 28s.*

Weber, Alfred. Farewell to European History: or The Conquest of Nihilism. *Translated from the German by R. F. C. Hull. 224 pp. 1947. 18s.*

SOCIOLOGY OF RELIGION

Argyle, Michael. Religious Behaviour. *224 pp. 8 figures. 41 tables. 1958. 25s.*

Knight, Frank H., and **Merriam, Thornton W.** The Economic Order and Religion. *242 pp. 1947. 18s.*

Watt, W. Montgomery. Islam and the Integration of Society. *320 pp. 1961. (2nd Impression.) 32s.*

SOCIOLOGY OF ART AND LITERATURE

Beljame, Alexandre. Men of Letters and the English Public in the Eighteenth Century: 1660-1744, Dryden, Addison, Pope. *Edited with an Introduction and Notes by Bonamy Dobree. Translated by E. O. Lorimer. 532 pp. 1948. 32s.*

Bruford, W. H. Chekhov and His Russia: a Sociological Study. *256 pp. 1948. 18s.*

Misch, Georg. A History of Autobiography in Antiquity. *Translated by E. W. Dickes. 2 Volumes. Vol. 1, 364 pp., Vol. 2, 372 pp. 1950. 45s. the set.*

SOCIOLOGY OF KNOWLEDGE

Hodges, H. A. The Philosophy of Wilhelm Dilthey. *410 pp. 1952. 30s.*

Mannheim, Karl. Essays on the Sociology of Knowledge. *Edited by Paul Kecskemeti. Editorial note by Adolph Lowe. 352 pp. 1952. (2nd Impression 1959.) 35s.*

Schlesinger, Rudolf. Marx: His Time and Ours. *464 pp. 1950. (2nd Impression 1951.) 32s.*

Stark, W. The History of Economics in its Relation to Social Development. *104 pp. 1944. (4th Impression 1957.) 12s.*
America: Ideal and Reality. The United States of 1776 in Contemporary Philosophy. *136 pp. 1947. 12s.*
The Sociology of Knowledge: An Essay in Aid of a Deeper Understanding of the History of Ideas. *384 pp. 1958. (2nd Impression 1960.) 36s.*
Montesquieu: Pioneer of the Sociology of Knowledge. *244 pp. 1960. 25s.*

URBAN SOCIOLOGY

Anderson, Nels. The Urban Community: A World Perspective. *532 pp. 1960. 35s.*

Ashworth, William. The Genesis of Modern British Town Planning: A Study in Economic and Social History of the Nineteenth and Twentieth Centuries. *288 pp. 1954. 25s.*

Cullingworth, J. B. Housing Needs and Planning Policy: A Restatement of the Problems of Housing Need and "Overspill" in England and Wales. *232 pp. 44 tables. 8 maps. 1960. 28s.*

Dickinson, Robert E. City Region and Regionalism: A Geographical Contribution to Human Ecology. *360 pp. 75 figures. 1947. (4th Impression 1960.) 25s.*
The West European City: A Geographical Interpretation. *600 pp. 129 maps. 29 plates. 2nd edition 1962. 55s.*

Dore, R. P. City Life in Japan: A Study of a Tokyo Ward. *498 pp. 8 plates. 4 figures. 24 tables. 1958. 45s.*

Glass, Ruth (Ed.). The Social Background of a Plan: A Study of Middlesbrough. *Preface by Max Lock. 298 pp. 37 tables. 21 folder maps and graphs in pocket. 1948. 42s.*

Gutkind, E. A. Revolution of Environment. *Demy 8vo. 476 pp. 32 plates. 60 figures. 3 folder maps. 1946. 32s.*

Jennings, Hilda. Societies in the Making: a Study of Development and Redevelopment within a County Borough. *Foreword by D. A. Clark. 286 pp. 1962. 32s.*

Kerr, Madeline. The People of Ship Street. *240 pp. 1958. 23s.*

Orlans, Harold. Stevenage: A Sociological Study of a New Town. *344 pp. 1 figure. 3 maps. 1952. 30s.*

RURAL SOCIOLOGY
(Demy 8vo.)

Bracey, H. E. English Rural Life: Village Activities, Organizations and Institutions. *302 pp. 1959. 30s.*

Infield, Henrik F. Co-operative Living in Palestine. *With a Foreword by General Sir Arthur Wauchope, G.C.B. 170 pp. 8 plates. 7 tables. 1946. 12s. 6d.*
Co-operative Communities at Work. *204 pp. 15 tables. 1947. 18s.*

Saville, John. Rural Depopulation in England and Wales, 1851-1951. *Foreword by Leonard Elmhirst. 286 pp. 6 figures. 39 tables. 1 map. 1957. 28s. (Dartington Hall Studies in Rural Sociology.)*

Williams, W. M. The Country Craftsman: A Study of Some Rural Crafts and the Rural Industries Organization in England. *248 pp. 9 figures. 1958. 25s. (Dartington Hall Studies in Rural Sociology.)*
The Sociology of an English Village: Gosforth. *272 pp. 12 figures. 13 tables. 1956. (2nd Impression 1956.) 25s.*

SOCIOLOGY OF MIGRATION
(*Demy 8vo.*)

Eisenstadt, S. N. The Absorption of Immigrants: a Comparative Study based mainly on the Jewish Community in Palestine and the State of Israel. *288 pp. 1954. 25s.*

Little, Dr. K. L. Negroes in Britain: A Study of Racial Relations in English Society. *320 pp. 1947. 25s.*

Richmond, Anthony H. Colour Prejudice in Britain: A Study of West Indian Workers in Liverpool, 1941-1951. *212 pp. 3 figures. 25 tables. 1954. 18s.*

SOCIOLOGY OF INDUSTRY AND DISTRIBUTION
(*Demy 8vo.*)

Anderson, Nels. Work and Leisure. *280 pp. 1961. 28s.*

Gouldner, Alvin W. Patterns of Industrial Bureaucracy. *298 pp. 1955. 21s.*
Wildcat Strike: A Study of an Unofficial Strike. *202 pp. 10 figures. 1955. 16s.*

Jefferys, Margot, with the assistance of Winifred Moss. Mobility in the Labour Market: Employment Changes in Battersea and Dagenham. *Preface by Barbara Wootton. 186 pp. 51 tables. 1954. 15s.*

Levy, A. B. Private Corporations and Their Control. *Two Volumes. Vol. 1, 464 pp., Vol. 2, 432 pp. 1950. 80s. the set.*

Levy, Hermann. The Shops of Britain: A Study of Retail Distribution. *268 pp. 1948. (2nd Impression 1949.) 21s.*

Liepmann, Kate. The Journey to Work: Its Significance for Industrial and Community Life. *With a Foreword by A. M. Carr-Saunders. 230 pp. 40 tables. 3 folders. 1944. (2nd Impression 1945.) 18s.*
Apprenticeship: An Enquiry into its Adequacy under Modern Conditions. *Foreword by H. D. Dickinson. 232 pp. 6 tables. 1960. (2nd Impression.) 23s.*

11

Smelser, Neil J. Social Change in the Industrial Revolution: An Application of Theory to the Lancashire Cotton Industry, 1770-1840. *468 pp. 12 figures. 14 tables. 1959. (2nd Impression 1960.) 40s.*

Williams, Gertrude. Recruitment to Skilled Trades. *240 pp. 1957. 23s.*

ANTHROPOLOGY
(*Demy 8vo.*)

Crook, David and **Isabel.** Revolution in a Chinese Village: Ten Mile Inn. *230 pp. 8 plates. 1 map. 1959. 21s.*

Dube, S. C. Indian Village, *Foreword by Morris Edward Opler. 276 pp. 4 plates. 1955. (4th Impression 1961.) 25s.*
India's Changing Villages: Human Factors in Community Development. *260 pp. 8 plates. 1 map. 1958. (2nd Impression 1960.) 25s.*

Fei, Hsiao-Tung. Peasant Life in China. *Foreword by Bronislaw Malinowski. 320 pp. 14 plates. 1939. (5th Impression 1962.) 30s.*

Fei, Hsiao-Tung and **Chang, Chih-I.** Earthbound China: A Study of Rural Economy in Yunnan. *Revised English edition prepared in collaboration with Paul Cooper and Margaret Park Redfield. 346 pp. 7 plates. 50 tables. 1948. 20s.*

Gulliver, P. H. The Family Herds. A Study of Two Pastoral Tribes in East Africa, The Jie and Turkana. *304 pp. 4 plates. 19 figures. 1955. 25s.*

Hogbin, Ian. Transformation Scene. The Changing Culture of a New Guinea Village. *340 pp. 22 plates. 2 maps. 1951. 30s.*

Hsu, Francis L. K. Under the Ancestors' Shadow: Chinese Culture and Personality. *346 pp. 26 figures. 1949. 21s.*
Religion, Science and Human Crises: A Study of China in Transition and its Implications for the West. *168 pp. 7 figures. 4 tables. 1952. 16s.*

Kelsen, Hans. Society and Nature: A Sociological Inquiry. *414 pp. 1946. 25s.*

Lin Yueh-Hwa. The Golden Wing: A Sociological Study of Chinese Familism. *Introduced by Raymond Firth. 264 pp. 1947. 18s.*

Lowie, Professor Robert H. Social Organization. *494 pp. 1950. (3rd Impression 1962.) 35s.*

Maunier, René. The Sociology of Colonies: An Introduction to the Study of Race Contact. *Edited and translated by E. O. Lorimer. 2 Volumes. Vol. 1, 430 pp., Vol. 2, 356 pp. 1949. 70s. the set.*

Mayer, Adrian C. Caste and Kinship in Central India: A Village and its Region. *328 pp. 16 plates. 15 figures. 16 tables. 1960. 35s.*
Peasants in the Pacific: A Study of Fiji Indian Rural Society. *232 pp. 16 plates. 10 figures. 14 tables. 1961. 35s.*

Osborne, Harold. Indians of the Andes: Aymaras and Quechuas. *292 pp. 8 plates. 2 maps. 1952. 25s.*

12

Smith, Raymond T. The Negro Family in British Guiana: Family Structure and Social Status in the Villages. *With a Foreword by Meyer Fortes. 314 pp. 8 plates. 1 figure. 4 maps. 1956. 28s.*

Yang, Martin C. A Chinese Village: Taitou, Shantung Province. *Foreword by Ralph Linton. Introduction by M. L. Wilson. 308 pp. 1947. 23s.*

DOCUMENTARY
(*Demy 8vo.*)

Belov, Fedor. The History of a Soviet Collective Farm. *250 pp. 1956. 21s.*

Meek, Dorothea L. (Ed.). Soviet Youth: Some Achievements and Problems. *Excerpts from the Soviet Press, translated by the editor. 280 pp. 1957. 28s.*

Schlesinger, Rudolf (Ed.). Changing Attitudes in Soviet Russia.
  1. The Family in the U.S.S.R. *Documents and Readings, with an Introduction by the editor. 434 pp. 1949. 30s.*
  2. The Nationalities Problem and Soviet Administration. Selected Readings on the Development of Soviet Nationalities Policies. *Introduced by the editor. Translated by W. W. Gottlieb. 324 pp. 1956. 30s.*

Reports
of the Institute
of Community Studies

(*Demy 8vo.*)

Jackson, Brian and **Marsden, Dennis.** Education and the Working Class: Some General Themes raised by a Study of 88 Working-class Children in a Northern Industrial City. *268 pp. 2 folders. 1962. 28s.*

Marris, Peter. Widows and their Families. *Foreword by Dr. John Bowlby. 184 pp. 18 tables. Statistical Summary. 1958. 18s.*
Family and Social Change in an African City. A Study of Rehousing in Lagos. *196 pp. 1 map. 4 plates. 53 tables. 1961. 25s.*

Mills, Enid. Living with Mental Illness: a Study in East London. *Foreword by Morris Carstairs. 196 pp. 1962. 28s.*

Townsend, Peter. The Family Life of Old People: An Inquiry in East London. *Foreword by J. H. Sheldon. 300 pp. 3 figures. 63 tables. 1957. (2nd Impression 1961.) 30s.*

Willmott, Peter and **Young, Michael.** Family and Class in a London Suburb. *202 pp. 47 tables. 1960. (2nd Impression 1961.) 21s.*

Young, Michael and **Willmott, Peter.** Family and Kinship in East London. *Foreword by Richard M. Titmuss. 252 pp. 39 tables. 1957.*

The **British Journal of Sociology.** *Edited by D. G. MacRae. Vol. 1, No. 1, March 1950 and Quarterly. Roy. 8vo., £2 12s. 6d. a number, post free. (Vols. 1-10, £3 each.)*

All prices are net and subject to alteration without notice